MW01595205

ANSWERS

TO UNANSWERED QUESTIONS

OF LIFE AND RELIGION

by Wm. Edwin Jacobs

Victory Publishing Company

Decatur, Illinois

ANSWERS TO UNANSWERED QUESTIONS
Of Life and Religion

Published by Victory Publishing Co., April 2006
First Printing, April 2006

Library of Congress
Control Number: 2006925517

For information or to purchase additional copies contact:
Victory Publishing Company
3797 N. Ashley Ct.
Decatur, IL 62526

(Cost: $14.00 per copy, plus $2.00 mailing within the U.S.A.)

ISBN: 0-9778925-0-6

*To
My wife Maria,
the love of my life.*

PREFACE

I am grateful to my professors, both at the Divinity School of Vanderbilt University (where I received a Master of Divinity Degree in 1976, and a Doctor of Ministry Degree in 1978) and to my professors at the St. Meinrad School of Theology at the Archabbey of St. Meinrad, where I spent my middler year studying for the Master of Divinity Degree. I am particularly indebted to my mentor, Professor Richard Wolf, at Vanderbilt who advised me throughout the degree programs; I remember him with fondness and gratitude for his friendship and the time he spent with me.

I owe a great deal of gratitude to my wife, Maria, who patiently and consistently encouraged me to write this book. I am also indebted to my brother, the Reverend Dale D. Jacobs and his wife Mary, for their essential help in proof-reading the manuscript. Many thanks also to Ben Edwin Crandall, my college classmate and life long friend, who also assisted in the proof reading.

The cover art work was created by Laura Podeschi, an upper division student in graphic arts at Millikin University.

All quotations from the Bible are from the NIV, unless otherwise indicated.

*For all men of that time lived and died by legend,
and without it the world hath become a mean place.*

from

<u>Arthur Rex: A Legendary Novel</u>
by Thomas Verger

CONTENTS

Introduction .... page 9

Question :
1.   Does a person have the right of self- 15
     defense? And if so, how far does the right go?

2.   Why, in the light of God's love, do we 22
     have to grow old?

3.   What part of our self lives on forever? 26

4.   What is God like? 31

5.   Is God male or female? 36

6.   Why is God silent and invisible? 38

7.   What constitutes saving faith? 41

8.   Which is correct, Creation or Evolution? 47

9.   In what ways are people equal? 52

10. Do both good and evil exist in the 55
     realm of the spirit?

11. Why is there a popular fascination with evil? . 62

12. Is there any reality to religious experience? 67

13. Why pray? Is there anything to prayer 76
     besides positive thinking?

14.   What is the purpose and use of meditation? 81

15.   What is sin? 84

16.   Is there really an unforgivable sin? 89

17.   Will God forgive us? On what conditions? 92
        Are we obligated to forgive each other?

18.   What happens at the time of death? 96

19.   Why did Jesus have to die? 99

20.   Why use bread and wine in communion? 101

21.   What is the Trinity? 106

22.   What will happen at the Last Judgment? 110

23.   What about people of other religions? 116

24.   Does God guard the lives of Christians? 119

25.   What is the status of children? 123

26.   Do the people of God undergo judgment? 127

27.   Why not just live ethically instead of 129
        being Christian?

28.   What is meant by the peace of God. 132

Projections of the future. 136

INTRODUCTION

"Everything nailed down is coming loose" in this world of accelerating change. And as the king is advised in Eugene Ionesco's play, *Exit the King,*

Snow is falling on the North Pole of the sun.
The Milky Way seems to be curdling.
> (*Exit the King.* Three Plays by
> Eugene Ionesco. New York:
> Grove Press, 1963. p. 17)

According to the hard sciences, the seemingly improbable is now being shown to be true. As a result the pleasure some people have in simply agonizing over critical questions is no longer tenable. People need answers, and they want them now, except, of course, people of a more negative mind-set.

In the fields of life and religion, and it seems in most areas of the social sciences, it is fashionable not to have answers to the really important questions in life. Evidently some think that to have a definite answer might be offensive to people of a different persuasion, or to those who have no answer at all. I suspect that some individuals really do not want to have an answer, but instead prefer to agonize over the question. However, by logic that is masochism. Yet it seems to be in several fields of learning; however, it is a sickness regardless of where you encounter it. The same can be said of the rigidity and legalism of those of the extreme right and the extreme left. It is interesting to note that both Europeans and Asians notice a masochistic tendency in the

American character. Presumably they would note that the U.S. was the first nation in history to go into war (the Vietnam War) determined not to win it. Naturally the other side won. The war was sold to the American people as a political war, but all wars are political. It is the logical equivalent of saying, "The blue sky is blue." War is far too serious for that kind of logic.

It is curious that the unwillingness to be decisive is usually found in people of a leftist bent of mind. It seems to occur in the social sciences, and particularly in religion. Whatever the field of learning or endeavor, the dysfunction exhibited in individuals is probably due to latent unresolved guilt, for which the individual seeks atonement by failure, trouble, or suffering. In that case, it probably is a vestige of historic Puritanism affecting the culture with the concept of works-righteousness for acceptance by God.

I use the term leftist because much of what passes for modern-day liberalism usually has little in common with classical liberalism, and the reason is that they violate the primary rule of liberalism in that they fail to question everything that comes down the road in the name of liberalism. To question everything was the historic manner of liberalism's pursuit of truth. Therefore Jesus was the true liberal; he went to the very heart and spirit of the Law.

Back in about 1980, I heard a lecture at the Divinity School of Vanderbilt University by the then editor of the Christian Century. He said that the growing power of the religious right was simply a natural reaction to what the liberal contingent had been doing all along, seeking social and political power. The reaction came because liberals had failed to follow the cardinal rule of liberalism, question everything, and they had not. They unquestioningly got on the band wagon of everything that came down the road in the name of liberalism, no matter how radical and outrageous.

During my career as the minister of several churches the questions to which I offer an answer in this book were frequently and privately asked; and upon answering them I was often urged to write down the answers and publish them. This venture might qualify as falling under the old saying, "Fools walk where angels fear to tread." But, the effort is worthwhile since it apparently meets a deep personal need of many people both in and out of the church.

One of the major problems in what passes for religious thinking today is that some who claim to be scholars are stuck in an outdated social concept of reality that is limited by a nineteenth century understanding of physical reality. They don't appear to be wide enough in their reading, or they didn't grasp the implications of modern concepts of physical reality (cosmology) where there are such bizarre conclusions as the fact, that has been proven, that the mass of an object increases increasingly proportional to the increase in the speed of that object. That is contrary to our normal common sense way of thinking, and yet the increase in mass can be read off the gauges of a cyclotron in the process of accelerating a particle. It is an example that shows that people tend to forget that "common sense" is society's composite learning from common experiences. But common sense, therefore, applies only to common experiences, not to uncommon experiences, such as the speeds reached in a cyclotron. At the speeds which we normally experience, the change in mass is too small to notice.

There are other things that have been proven which seem totally contrary to common sense. One is that increasingly proportional to the increase in the speed of an object, time slows down. And it was during the latter half of the 20th-century that one scientist proved that there is just barely a slight forward bias in time; in other words, there is no danger of time reversing and history unraveling backwards.

It often is the anomaly in experimental results, data that is different from the rest, that leads to important breakthroughs. It really is a strange world we live in. Or to put it as Albert Einstein did when he criticized the phenomenon of "entanglement", "It is spooky action at a distance." But then it was shown to be true by experiments. When you add to that the modern bizarre concepts of chaos and randomness in the universe, it really is a strange world. But some people are stuck in the social concept of physical reality of the 19th century, which was primarily dominated by Newtonian physics. Unfortunately, a lack of understanding of modern epistemology, or else a regrettable not keeping up with recent developments in scientific thought limited their vision.

In one upper division engineering sequence math course, the professor warned us not to rely on common sense; it would lead us wrong because we would be dealing with nth-dimensional systems, beyond the range of common sense [and common experience]. Also, I think the origin of the concept of natural law seems to have come out of the covenant God made after the flood, recorded in the Book of Genesis (8:20-22; 9:8-17). It was passed on and elaborated by Western culture and science. However, in our day scientists typically speak of natural consistencies rather than natural law. As a result, what is normally described as a miracle is within the realm of possibility as far as today's science is concerned.

It is interesting to note at this point that the foundation of Christianity, the one rock upon which it rests, is the historical event of the resurrection of Jesus Christ. Professor John Killinger said, "Every major religion is based on magic in its origin." Certainly the resurrection of Jesus is a supernatural event any way you look at it. Once you have granted the truth of the resurrection of Jesus, then you have in principle granted the possibility of other miracles, such as those reported in the New Testament Scriptures.

In regard to the New Testament Scriptures, I have found it curious that the Twelve Disciples are often considered to be ignorant peasants, incapable of writing, and yet at least several of them were business men and at least one was a tax collector, all of which presumed the capability of writing. It would be bizarre, and has to be in the realm of high improbability, if none of them ever wrote down during their own lifetime the story of the life of Jesus on earth, his teachings and actions. It seems inconceivable, unless a person proposing such an idea is consciously intent on undercutting the authority of the Scriptures. Yet such presumptions are often proposed as scholarly findings, whereas they actually are biased opinion because there is no valid proof from the person making the claim, only a heuristic appeal. It is legitimate to say that such an approach is a faith position that is part of the social concept of reality characteristic of a bygone era. On the other hand, there is an old saying: "The word of God is to you whatever you want it to be." And that is the judgment of it.

I have eaten your bread and salt;
I have drunk your water and wine.
The deaths ye died I have watched beside,
And the lives ye led were mine.

by Rudyard Kipling

ONE

DOES A PERSON HAVE THE RIGHT OF SELF-DEFENSE?

AND IF SO, HOW FAR DOES THIS RIGHT GO?

This is a paramount question of our time. The straight answer is yes! That is true even in both the Old Testament and New Testament Scriptures, and the extent a person can go is taking a life, if it is necessary in order to save your own life or that of others. It is interesting to note that Malachi Martin stated in one of his books that the difference between self-defense and murder is the thought in the mind of the one who does it. In other words, another person with a different vantage point might possibly come to a different conclusion based on a different set of data, and see it as an unnecessary or inappropriate response.

The prohibition in the sixth commandment of the Ten Commandments is a prohibition against murder, but not killing. The correct translation of the word in its original usage is murder, according to one scholar, Professor Walter Harrelson at Vanderbilt University. He participated in the translation of the Revised Standard Version of the Bible. In his book, The Ten Commandments and Human Rights, he noted that the only time a person can justifiably take a life is as an agent of God, or in self-defense, or in protecting others. The Bible, from cover to cover, acknowledges that right.

We find the ancient right of self-defense endorsed in the Old Testament very early. It was first mentioned in the "Song of the Sword," which is the story of Lamech in the fourth chapter of Genesis, verses 23-24.

> Adah and Zillah, listen to me,
> wives of Lamech, hear my words.
> I have killed a man for wounding me,
> a young man for injuring me.
> If Cain is avenged seven times,
> then Lamech seventy-seven times.

It is an allusion to the story of Cain and Abel, which occurs earlier in the fourth chapter. After God confronts Cain with his deed and announces his punishment, Cain states that his punishment is more than he can bear; anybody who finds him will kill him.

> But the Lord said to him, "Not so; if anyone kills Cain, he will suffer vengeance seven times over." Then the Lord put a mark on Cain so that no one who found him would kill him.   (4:15)

The extreme difference in the vengeance vowed underlines that the killing by Lamech in self-defense was justified, whereas Cain's act was not justified.

When we turn to the New Testament teachings, we are mindful that for nearly all of us who are of Christian faith, regardless of denominational persuasion, we nearly all recognize the twenty-seven books of the New Testament as Scripture, canon of truth, and rule of faith. Such recognition was made official policy by the ecumenical councils of the church under the guidance of the Holy Spirit. The last truly ecumenical council of the church was at Chalcedon in 451 A.D. Furthermore, the accepted twenty-seven books of the New Testament have been endorsed by the church universal through the centuries. They are one unified body of truth, and are our handrail in the dark when we deal with the realm of the spirit.

When we consider the New Testament, we find that Jesus said to his disciples at the Last Supper, as recorded in the Gospel According to St. Luke,

> "When I sent you without purse, bag or sandals, did you lack anything?"
> "Nothing," they answered.
> He said to them, "But now if you have a purse, take it, and also a bag; and if you don't have a sword, sell your cloak and buy one."   (22:35-36)

From those parting instructions it seems likely that many of the martyrdoms by execution were after the fight. After all, they had the right of self defense, but not the right to initiate aggression.

It is an easy thing to see that the right of self-defense applies to the protection of others on an individual basis, but when it comes to the application of it on a massive, and consequentially impersonal, scale in warfare, the application of the principle becomes more complicated, if for no other reason than that the power drive of a national leader may lead him, or her, to exaggerate or falsify the information given out to the people. However, the principle of the right of self-defense still applies as the right to the defense of one's own nation, and to the defense of other nations also threatened. War is a horrible thing, but as a last resort for defense, it can be just. Two modern day examples of that are Adolf Hitler and the one who held Hitler as a role model, Saddam Hussein, who also was known as "the Butcher of Baghdad." His goal evidently was to re-establish the Persian Empire of antiquity, with himself as world, or at least regional, ruler. During World War II an estimated total of forty million people died on both sides, a tragedy the likes of which the world had never seen before, nor imagined. During and after that war the allied leaders wished they had stopped Hitler earlier, for he continued on the road of expansionism despite Neville Chamberlain's warning, "You will set all Europe aflame." The people of Iraq and of the world are far better off without "the Butcher of Baghdad" ruling in a world containing increasing numbers and varieties of weapons of mass destruction.

St. Paul wrote of the role of the national ruler, and his right to use the sword, lethal force, in defense of order and security of the people.

> For he is God's servant to do you good. But if you do wrong, be afraid, for he does not bear the sword for nothing.   (Romans 13:4)

But when he does not act as God's servant, allegiance or obedience is not owed. Two easy examples are Adolf Hitler and Saddam Hussein.

It was predicted by one notable man in 1904 that the twentieth century would be characterized by volcanic change, and it turned out to be true. Unfortunately the twenty-first century could easily become known in retrospect as the century of genocide, as well as of increasingly rapid technological progress. It is interesting to note that the twentieth century was the one first characterized by sudden death, accidental and intentional, whereas in earlier times a person usually had time to set his house in order. I think there were more people killed by violence in the twentieth century than in all of previously recorded history. One is reminded that according to the theory of evolution, mankind came on the scene as an armed killer. It is ironic that the oldest known, intact human corpse was killed by an arrow. The 10,000 year old corpse, named "the Ice man," was found in a glacier in the Italian Alps. When you consider the whole story of creation, mankind has fallen downward, not upwards. As one poet put it, "The leaves have fallen, and so has mankind."

In the account of Lawrence of Arabia, one time he led Arab troops in an attack on an enemy troop train; when the enemy troops surrendered, he showed extraordinary mercy on all of the prisoners. He had the wounded treated, the others disarmed, and all of them set free. But at the next battle, he had all of the captives killed. A reporter who was traveling with the army, went to the sheik who was the actual ruler of the territory, and the army drawn from it. The reporter asked the sheik how Lawrence could be so merciful after the first battle, but was absolutely bloodthirsty after the second battle. The sheik answered, "With Lawrence, mercy is a matter of emotion, but with me mercy is a matter of good manners. Judge for yourself which is more dependable." Our will must be dominant over our emotions. Therefore, using feelings as the primary factor in decisions can easily be a sure route to trouble in some cases, and even to jail. The reason is feelings are a composite response made up of the emotion of the moment, inherited temperament, personal history, IQ, and the make-up of the external situation. Consequently, situation ethics as a national philosophy and policy is a prescription for social disorder, as the current state of the world demonstrates. There has been an unfortunate leveling down in morality of American society and elsewhere, rather than leveling up. This has happened since the removal of all controls on the media. The social engineers who arranged it were either incredibly naïve about human nature, or else of evil inclination to the point of nihilism.

There is an extreme seriousness in the several genocides of the twentieth century. When Adolf Eichmann was captured and brought to trial in Israel, it was determined that a witness was necessary to identify him as the one who was in charge of the death camp. When the witness, who was a very elderly man, was brought into the court room, and saw Eichmann for the first time that close, he screamed and fainted. When he regained consciousness they asked him why he reacted that way. He answered, "I was expecting a half god." When he saw that Eichmann was only human, he realized that we all are capable of such evil, and that it could happen again and again. What the future might hold was too much for him. And genocide has happened repeatedly since

World War II, and with little or no action by the United Nations organization.

November 11, 1918 was the day the Armistice ending World War I took effect. The ceasefire was to begin at 11:00 A.M. on the 11th day of the 11th month of the year 1918, thereby ending World War I. One soldier who was on the front line during that time later wrote that just prior to the ceasefire, both the Allied and German soldiers turned their guns toward the sky and fired off their remaining ammunition so that the fighting could not resume. He said that when the firing ceased at 11:00 A.M., the silence fell like the voice of God. It isn't often today that a person hears the voice of God. (Of course, in Jewish tradition one does not hear the voice of God directly and live; a person hears the "echo of the Divine voice," the "daughter of the voice.")

In our own day the 3,000 year old conflict between barbarism and civilization has spread to the United States. Our enemies are within the gates, a 5th column within. Therefore we dare not lose in this conflict between good and evil, between civilization and terrorism. History has shown that to delay, and act late on the urgent expediency of the moment, multiplies the death and suffering. For example, Adolf Hitler should have been stopped at the first sign of aggression. As it is, this man who came out of nowhere has affected history for centuries to come. He taught by example how far evil can go. We dare not forget that bitter lesson. In the current conflict between civilization and terrorism, to "cut and run" is to lose our freedom, our heritage, and to lose an incredible number of lives.

I would wish for you the world
If it were good enough for you.

by Rod McKuen

TWO

WHY, IN THE LIGHT OF GOD'S LOVE, DO WE HAVE TO GROW OLD?

Sooner or later nearly everybody asks that question of God or life, either consciously or subconsciously - because of the illnesses, disabilities, and frailties that to some degree usually come with aging - and it makes a world of difference what answer you come up with. Some people are embittered in their later years by the status of their health, of their finances, or their way of life. I remember one elderly lady in a nursing home that I frequently visited as Minister of the church. She sat in the lounge every day with her small suitcase close at hand waiting for her family to come and take her home. The tragedy is that this has happened in many people's lives –people left alone to grieve in their later years.

There is an Oriental belief that life is divided into three phases, each of them is approximately 20 years in length. The first phase is that of coming-of-age, which involves school. The second phase is raising a family and having a career. The third phase is the reflective process of integrating life. That last phase is crucial; it is a matter of making sense out of all that has happened in life. It is an intermittent, long stroll down memory lane.

Consequently, what often passes for dementia in persons who are elderly is in reality a redirection of attention from the present time events to the events in the past, 20, 30, 40, or 50 years. They simply are not paying attention to the events happening around them in the present time, and therefore they can't remember what day it is, or who visited them yesterday. In such cases the cure, or treatment, is to insist that they also focus on the present day events, so that they can live today as well as relive and integrate those yesterdays.

If we all lived in perfect health always, with no diminishing of capability with age, and then after some approximate number of years died, with no real pain or suffering, then we really would have to be dragged kicking and screaming into the next phase of life. And there would be even more hatred of God, more rebellion than now. Since every body would be self-sufficient, we wouldn't need anybody else. That would be a guaranteed prescription for anarchy and war. That really would be hell on earth, especially since there would be no really true need for love, or at least no opportunity to practice sacrificial love, therefore I doubt that it would exist.

As it is, the process of aging can be thought of as nature's way of taking life in this material phase away from us a little bit at a time, until we are ready to take God up on the next phase of life, totally in the spiritual dimension of reality, with a new spiritual body, one no longer subject to pain, decay, disease, and death. St. Paul wrote that it will be as much greater than this material body as a tree is greater than the seed that it comes from. (cf. I Corinthians 15:36-58) As some note, the transition event is a promotion, at least for those who are "right with God."

Some years ago there was a motion picture that came out with the title, *Death Takes a Holiday*. In that story the angel of death decides to take three days off and go to earth in the guise of a man to find out why people hold onto life persistently even in the face of great suffering. During his time off there is great misery throughout the world because people who need to be released from their suffering can find no release by death.

But the interesting thing is where Mr. Death goes for his vacation. He crashes a family reunion on an island estate, where the patriarch of the family is an elderly gentleman who is confined to a wheel chair, unable to walk. Finally, the man recognizes Mr. Death, and privately confronts him, demanding to know why he has come there. After Mr. Death explains his quest, and asks why he holds onto life tightly despite the pain; why not turn loose of life on this earth that involves such great pain. And the elderly gentleman states, "I stand it!" Mr. Death responds, "Even if I can assure you eternal life in heaven?" The gentleman rejects the offer of an immediate transition, and defiantly states, "I stand the pain! I stand it, because everything I know and love is here!"

There is another reason, also, for the slings and arrows of outrageous fortune in the so-called "golden years", in which ironically many people find a distinct short-age of tangible gold. Suffering and trouble, properly borne, builds moral character. (cf, Hebrews 12:1-13) It builds moral character by breaking down pride, which is the basis of all sin. But if such challenges are improperly borne – without humility and repentance – then they can destroy a person's character through bitterness, resentment, and hatred. After all, God's primary interest seems to be in building moral character, and not in making us comfortable.

The Christian religion is something simple and sublime.
It means one thing, and one thing only, Eternal life lived in
the midst of time, by the strength and under the eyes of God.

by Adolf Harnack, <u>What Is Christianity?</u>
New York: Harper &Row, Publishers, 1957. p. 8

THREE

WHAT PART OF YOU
LIVES ON ETERNALLY?

Usually, when questioned, people have a more or less undefined concept of self, sort of like a kernel of life, that they think lives on eternally. The words typically used to express that part of the self are called "soul" (pseukhe, in the Greek language) or "spirit" (pneuma, in the Greek). "Pseukhe" refers to "the life force, the thinking, willing, feeling" aspect of the individual. And "pneuma" refers to "the breath of life, the thinking, willing, feeling" aspect of the individual. If you notice the commonality there is between the two words, the major factors that they hold in common are thinking, willing, feeling. That combination of words, we would today call personality. Now, it is true that St. Paul used the word spirit in the Greek sense of the word as the refined part of the soul that is capable of apprehending God. But the common use was, as in the Gospel accounts, where the two words were used interchangeably. Therefore it is the personality that lives on eternally.

This has interesting ramifications because it means that in one sense that each person is building a life history, or to put it another way, life isn't anything except opportunity. It is the opportunity to be something, to do something. But the important thing is each person is shaping his life history, and consequently the kind of person he is in the process of becoming, and that will live on forever. In the process, a person must remember the analogy of the human mind to a computer in some respects, and as a result, "Garbage in equals garbage out." In other words, choose carefully the experiences and information that you put into your mind, for it will shape you and your actions. Business and industry spend billions of dollars per year on that proven principle, in the money spent on television advertising – the images and words have a proven affect on behavior, motivating individuals to buy the product or service. A person, therefore, should choose his friends and experiences as carefully as possible.

It is an interesting sidelight to the mention of the realm of the spirit that there is another word in the Greek, "phantasma", from which we get the English word "phantom." When the Twelve disciples were in a boat, crossing the Sea of Galilee and a storm came up, and Jesus came to them walking on the water, at first they identified what they saw as a "phantasma", or apparition, and from a distance it kind of looked like Jesus. When they called out, "Lord, is it you?" He answered with a mind jarring and terrifying phrase, which literally translated from the Greek is, "I am!" It was the phrase used as the identifying name of God given to Moses for use when the Israelites asked who sent him to liberate them. By Hebrew tradition, no person sees God and lives. The Disciples thought they were about to die. The subsequent events of the story tell of the awe they had for this Jesus who calmed the wind and the waves with just a word.

But there still remains a vital question regarding the self that lives on into the next phase of life for eternity. Which you lives on? Is it yourself as you were at the age of 15 years old, or 20 years old, or 35, or 50, or 72, or 85? Lawrence LeShan examined this question very intensely and he came up with the conclusion that I believe is true, and which is in accord with religious experience. The dominant time of consciousness as you make that transition to the next phase of life, is the time in this phase of your life when you were most aware of the reality of the world around you in both its material and spiritual dimensions. All the other times in your life are there in conscious memory. You don't lose anything as far as perceptions of this world are concerned.

When a Christian makes the transition to next phase of life and the blessings it involves, the timing is another interesting question. The answer from experience seems to be, when it is the best for all concerned in the perspective of eternity. There seems to be another factor involved: when the individual peaks out in spiritual development. Both of those probably are involved in the third and deciding factor, the will of God in all of his infinite wisdom and mercy.

From the resurrection appearances of Jesus, we know that we will be recognizable, and no longer bound by materiality or time as we know it. As the Apostle John wrote,

> Dear friends, now we are the children of God, and
> what we will be has not yet been made known. But
> we know that when he appears, we shall be like him,
> for we shall see him as he is.   (I John 3:2)

It should be noted also for consideration that St.
Thomas Acquinas stated that the separated soul is woefully
incomplete without its separated body. That will be reme-
died, at the time of the last judgment, with a spiritual body
far superior to this material one – no longer subject to pain,
decay, disease, death, or even aging.

One time I visited a man in the hospital who was a
former U.S.A.F. fighter pilot who flew P-51 Mustangs during World War II in the European Theater. Having seen
many news reels, I asked him when the planes went in to
strafe, why did the pilots wing their planes over up-side-
down, using hard right aileron, and then dive to the attack?
He said he didn't know. All he knew was that they were
ordered to do it. The maneuver was known as a "split S."

It occurred to me that if a pilot simply dove to the
attack, all he could see was what was ahead of him. But if
he winged the plane over until it was up-side-down, then all
of the terrain from horizon to horizon would be spread out
above his head. He then could pick out the target and dive
to the attack.

Analogously, in a manner of speaking, when we
open our lives to the Spirit of God, and open our minds to
the world in all of its reality – both spiritual and material –
then we can accurately focus in on our destiny with God.
Remembering also that as Viktor Frankl stated, "The past is

the treasure house of accomplishments, and the present is the opportunity to redeem the mistakes of the past." This world is a moral training ground for this phase of life. Life is really just opportunity. Along the way in our pilgrimage into the future we have to deal with that deadly triad: suffering, guilt, and death. The Christian gospel offers deliverance from death and guilt now, and in the next phase of life, deliverance from suffering. And isn't it true that as Alexander Pope wrote,

> You purchase pain with all that joy can give,
> and die of nothing but a rage to live.

From, "Moral Essays" II, XCVII

A.M.D.G.

Ad Majorum Dei Gloriam.
"For the greater glory of God."

motto of the Jesuits

FOUR

WHAT IS GOD LIKE?

Today there are all kinds of answers to that question. And many people get all of their information from motion pictures and television programs about the realm of the spirit. On the other hand, there is the innocence of childhood. I once asked a five year old girl what she thought God looked like; her answer was, "He is an elderly man with a long white beard, and he is sitting in a lawn chair."

Actually there are some things that we can know from nature about God. Nature certainly witnesses to a supreme, intelligent Creator. Using what is called a heuristic argument, which is an appeal to reason, a prime example of it is called the watchmaker theory. If a person who has never seen a pocket watch is walking along and comes upon a pocket watch and examines it, and notes the order and precision of it, then he would conclude that this instrument did not come together by accident, and that someplace there must be a watchmaker. Likewise, by reasoning we conclude, as a result of the complexity of the world around us, that somewhere there must be a world maker. St. Paul, in the first chapter of his letter to the Romans, uses that argument to assert the existence and power of God.

But there is another thing we can know from nature about God. It comes from the theology of the High Middle Ages. It is the principle that in every aspect of creation there is some vestige of the Creator. All artists convey their own particular style, however subtle, upon their work of art. It is by that distinctive manner of painting, or what-ever their medium of art, that their identity, and even their existence, is confirmed. By such a shortcut analogy, the same is true of God.

Another conclusion that we can draw from the world about us is that God loves variety. Note that there is an interesting uniqueness to everything about us in the world, and especially in people; each one is a very special person – as indicated by DNA, the retina, and fingerprints.

When we turn to the Scriptures, from cover to cover in the Bible, there is the consistent theme of God's love for people. We notice it in the murder of Abel by his brother Cain. In the story of that terrible act, the mark put on Cain was a mark of protection by God. That is extraordinary mercy considering the crime. (cf. Genesis 4:1-16) In the story of Sodom and Gomorrah (Genesis 18:1 to 19:29), Abraham bargains with God to spare the cities if there are just 50 righteous people in those cities; for the sake of those 50 surely he would not destroy the city.

> Will you sweep away the righteous with the wicked? What if there are fifty righteous people in the city? Will you really sweep it away and not spare the place for the sake of the fifty righteous people in it? Far be it from you to do such a thing – to kill the righteous with the wicked, treating the righteous and the wicked alike. Far be it from you. Will not the judge of all the earth do right?   (Genesis 18:24-25)

Abraham bargained God down to 45, then 40, 30, 20, and finally 10 righteous people. For the sake of those 10 righteous people he would not destroy the cities. However, he didn't get near the number 4, which was the number of people in Lot's family. Therefore, there is something far more important involved here than saving Lot's family. Evidently Abraham was trying to establish what the basic inclination of God is, to save or to destroy.

God's love for his people is affirmed throughout the Old Testament by the prophets. And in the New Testament the primary theme is God's love for people, as is witnessed by that famous verse John 3:16. In the English language we have only one word for the various concepts of love, whereas in the ancient Greek language in which the New Testament was written, there were four different words for the four different kinds of love. The one used in the New Testament Scriptures of Christian love for one another, and for God, and vice versa, is "agape" which means essentially in straight English "unwillingness to do without." Notice that it is a will-centered response, and consequently it can be commanded, as Jesus did – towards God and neighbor. In the Parable of the Good Samaritan he illustrated and defined neighbor as anybody you meet, regardless of religion, nationality, or race. To love everybody in the whole wide world seems to be an impossible task; as a law it seems impossible to obey, and only serves as pious PR. But when you confine the law of love to neighbor, and define neighbor as someone you have met, then it is possible to be "unwilling to do without" them. This can be true if the meeting or contact is in person or through some medium, such as telephone or television news reports of people in need. The contact establishes an obligation.

From a Christian perspective, "What is God like?" is an easy question to answer, for it tells in the letter to the Hebrews (1:1-4), in the New Testament Scriptures, that Jesus is the exact image of God. In speaking of Jesus, verse 1:3 states that,

> The Son is the radiance of God's glory and the exact representation of his being, sustaining all things by his powerful word.

The interesting thing about that quotation is that not only is he the exact image of God, but that if you would like to know what God is like, then read the Gospel accounts of the life of Jesus on earth. God, the Father Almighty, is just that kind and good. There is another interesting item in that verse. In it, this material universe, as we know it, is not able to exist one moment more except by Jesus' permission. That is the power of the risen and ruling Christ. Notice also that in the first two verses provision is made for other religions; God spoke "through the prophets at many times and in various ways", but now in this time he has spoken through his Son, who is heir of all things and through whom the universe was created.

There are also other aspects of God that are windows into what he is like, such as "righteousness" (being such as one ought to be) and "merciful", but the primary mode is love. One caution though, he is streetwise to a hustle.

There will be no winner in the war between the sexes, because there is too much fraternization between the combatants.

Source unknown

FIVE

IS GOD MALE OR FEMALE?

It seems to me there is a certain amount of frivolity to the question, for the answer seems obvious. Neither! Human sexuality is a thing unique to this world of materiality. Theologians of the past assumed that this was realized and started beyond that point. In the Gospel according to St. Matthew 22:23-32 Jesus confronted the question of marriage in the resurrection by his answer to the story of a woman who successively was the wife of seven brothers. As each brother died childless by her, she would be married to the next one, in accordance with the law, to raise a child for the first husband. And in Jesus' answer to the question of which one she will be married to in the resurrection, he stated:

> At the resurrection people will neither marry nor be given in marriage; they will be like the angels in heaven.   (Matthew 22:29)

It is true that the basic function or activity of God is that of creativity, and therefore because of the fact that the woman bears children, it seems she is more akin to the basic nature of God than a man is. A person could naturally ask that if the basic nature of God has that commonality by virtue of function, then why wasn't the term mother used for God? Yet they deliberately, by their choice, referred to him as God the Father. There is a very good reason for that, and it holds as true today as it did then. The word father still indicates the role of "protector, upholder, sustainer." All of these were functions of a father in the time of Jesus, and they hold true throughout recorded human history. Furthermore, those have always been characteristics of God the Father Almighty and therefore the title still remains appropriate.

Ah, but a man's reach should exceed his grasp,
or what's a heaven for?

by Robert Browning, Andrea del Sarto

SIX

WHY IS GOD SILENT AND INVISIBLE?

The reason is to preserve the free will of people, free to go our own chosen way in life. In the Genesis account of creation (chapters one and two), mankind was created for fellowship with God, a voluntary fellowship. However, if God spoke or appeared occasionally to all people, either individually or in groups, there would be an obvious compulsion to follow the dictates of God; it would not be an entirely voluntary fellowship. It would be a biased situation.

Of course, contrary to that, a person could cite the example of Thomas, one of the inner group of Twelve Disciples. He was not with the other Disciples in the upper room on Easter evening when the resurrected Jesus appeared to them.

> When the other disciples told him that they had seen the Lord, he declared, "Unless I see the nail marks in his hands and put my finger where the nails were, and put my hand into his side, I will not believe it."
> (John 20:25)

For Doubting Thomas, as subsequent generations

have called him, such high quality testimony, as the disciples gave, was not enough. Dead is dead! And Jesus' crucifixion after being kept up all night with trials, and beaten nearly to death before being nailed to the cross, was a sure way to become dead. Thomas must have seen the crucifixion of Jesus.

> A week later his disciples were in the house again, and Thomas was with them. Though the doors were locked, Jesus came and stood among them and said,
>
> "Peace be with you!" Then he said to Thomas, "Put your finger here and see my hands. Reach out your hand and put it into my side. Stop doubting and believe."
>
> Thomas said to him, "My Lord and my God!"
>
> Then Jesus told him, "Because you have seen me, you have believed; blessed are those who have not seen and yet have believed."
> (John 20:26-29)

Notice his pronouncement of blessing upon us who have believed because of the call to faith passed on by the Twelve Disciples, who were commissioned by Jesus as Apostles after his resurrection. Remember also that the primary function of the Twelve Apostles was to be witnesses of the resurrection. (Acts 1:21-22) Therefore Thomas' demand was honored.

But I believe there was another dynamic also at work. Jesus "owed him one." Just before their current trip to Jerusalem, while they were beyond the Jordan River and in a foreign country, not under the jurisdiction of Judah or Israel, Jesus received a message that his friend Lazarus was ill. Knowing that Lazarus was dying, Jesus waited two more days before starting the journey to him. Jesus delayed deliberately so that there would be no question of Lazarus being dead. That was necessary in order to establish the validity of the resurrection of Lazarus. The extent of the time in the tomb (4 days) would rule out a resuscitation.

As Jesus and his disciples were about to start the last journey to Jerusalem,

> Then Thomas (called Didymus) said to the rest of the disciples "Let us also go, that we may die with him."
> (John 11:16)

There already must have been an arrest warrant out for Jesus. Thomas rallied the troops, so to speak. Therefore to put it in modern jargon, Jesus owed Thomas one (favor). None of us has that kind of handle on Jesus. That is why we cannot demand an epiphany in like manner.

Reporter: *"Can you give us a one sentence summary of your theology?"*

Answer: *Yes! It is in one of your gospel songs:*
             "Jesus loves me, this I know, for the Bible tells me so."

> Karl Barth, upon his arrival in the U.S. for a lecture series.

SEVEN

FAITH: IN CHRISTIANITY, WHAT CONSTITUTES SAVING FAITH?

Hurrying through what can be a tedious subject, dry as a flower pressed between the pages of a Bible, faith is easy to define biblically, for a definition of it occurs in the New Testament Scriptures, in which the word "hope" is used with the religious meaning of certainty, and not in the secular sense of the word which indicates doubt (about at the level of wishing upon a star). "Now faith is being sure of what we hope for and certain of what we do not see." (Hebrews 11:1) When a person speaks of saving faith there are a number of aspects to that. Note that the only place where the phrase "by faith alone" occurs is James 2:24, where it denies that salvation is by faith alone. Christian faith involves more than intellectual assent to the truth of the gospel; it involves the commitment of the will to the point of action in accordance with the commitment. As St. James notes:

> You believe that there is one God, Good! Even the demons believe that and shudder.

> You foolish man, do you want evidence that faith without deeds is useless?
>
> (James 2:19-20)

Some would object that is too legalistic and rigid to be consistent with the teachings of Jesus, and yet Jesus is recorded as saying, "Not everyone who says to me, 'Lord, Lord,' will enter the kingdom of heaven, but only he who does the will of my Father who is in heaven." (Matthew 7:21) It matches the admonition by the prophets in the Old Testament: "Fear God, and keep his commandments." That is just another way of saying, "Worship God, and lead a moral life."

Actually, there are listed in Scripture five different things that bring salvation. So, which is it? It is all five together: faith (John 3:16), repentance (II Corinthians 7:10), confession (Romans 10:10), baptism (I Peter 3:21), and living by the will of God (Matthew 7:21; James 2:18-19, 26). In other words, faith - both intellectual assent to the truth of the gospel, plus commitment of the will – must be of such integrity that it shows itself in each of those actions, prompted by the will. Some denominations specialize in just one of those vestiges of faith.

In summary of Jesus' teachings about the way to life eternal with God, it comes down to this: the basic orientation of a person's life must be the kingdom of God – the rule of God in his life. In essence that is, live by the Greatest Commandment, the love for God, and by the Second Commandment, to love your neighbor as yourself. (Matthew 22:34-40; Mark 12:28-34; Luke 10:25-28) In the parable of the Good Samaritan (Luke 10:29-37), your neighbor is defined as anybody you meet, regardless of race, ethnic origin, or religion. Faith must be the central dynamic of life, and then that is the saving faith. It is the unconditional love for God and others, and in the sense of sacrificial living. It is the taking up the cross and following Jesus - to be just that kind and good.

There is one caution that should be noted, for I think many people have fallen victim of it, apostasy – a willful turning from the faith. The writer of the Letter to the Hebrews records,

> It is impossible for those who have once been enlightened, who have tasted the heavenly gift, who have shared in the Holy Spirit, who have tasted the goodness of the word of God and the powers of the coming age, if they fall away, to be brought back to repentance, because to their loss they are crucifying the Son of God all over again and subjecting him to public disgrace.   (6:4-6)

That is the chilling reminder of the seriousness of a person's involvement in the kingdom of God. In effect it says, don't let the door hit you in the back on the way out. In the Greek text it appears to be indiscernible what bars their returning to the faith: God, or their prior experience has inoculated them against faith.

On the positive side, the ritual of baptism, is the formal entrance into the Christian life, for it functions as a marker in history. At that event there are, as gifts from God, the following benefits: Forgiveness for all prior sins now (rather than going to Hades to await the Last Judgment on a gamble); adoption as a son or daughter of God; the dwelling within of the Holy Spirit; the presence of God and his blessing throughout life; and when it comes time to enter the next phase of life there is an immediate entrance into heaven for eternity rather than going to Hades (the place of the dead); and finally a new spiritual body, one no longer subject to pain, decay, disease, and death. As a personal destiny it wins first prize.

In the rampant, self entertainment life style of people today, where it seems like the role of conduct and communication has gone to the lowest common denominator among many people, there is a caution that comes to us in Scripture of the seriousness of the nature of the call to the life of faith. On one occasion Jesus told the Parable of the Narrow Gate. He said:

> Enter by the narrow gate; for the gate is wide and the way in is easy that leads to destruction, and those who enter by it are many. For the gate is narrow and the way is hard that leads to life, and those who find it are few.
>
> (Matthew 7:13-14)

It reminds me of the line of poetry that reads:

> The sharp edge of a razor is hard to pass over, thus sayeth the wise, the road to eternity is hard.

It takes a real serious endeavor to respond properly to the Divine gift that we have been given, for the opportunity of eternal life with God.

On the other hand, in his great love for mankind, God is very receptive to our feeble efforts. I remember the case of a woman who, while she was being operated on, was holding a conversation with Jesus. But the doctor was hearing only one side of the conversation and it was unnerving him. During her discussion with Jesus, she asked him, "Is the Baptist church the true church?" And the answer that came back was so profound that it could not have come from her. This must certainly have been a genuine religious experience, for the answer was: "It is the right church for you at this time in your life."

Of course there is the Parable of the Talents (Matthew 25:14-30) where it is just a coincidence of language that "talent" in the English language refers to the human capacity in one activity. Whereas, in the Greek language of that time, a talent was the largest denomination of weight of gold used as money. And so they had no direct connection.

In the story, a man was going on a long journey, and he left his wealth in the care of three servants, the first one with five talents, the second with two talents, and the third was given the care of one talent. The first two invested their shares and doubled the amounts that they were entrusted with. The third hid his one talent and gave it back intact, but with no increase. Jesus spoke of him as being sent to the outer darkness, hell. Allegorically, the moral is that he had failed to fully use his God given share, his abilities (talents). According to that we are all going to hell.

But, the direct meaning is that the unworthy servant failed to increase his share in the Kingdom of God, an opportunity that was placed in his care. Likewise, we are under the same obligation, namely to progress in the faith, to grow in understanding, love, and charitable action in the Kingdom of God. It is a critical mistake to be Christian in name only. As Professor James Glasse use to say: "Being a Christian is a little like being pregnant in one way. You either are, or aren't. You can't be a little bit pregnant." Our obligation must always be seen in the perspective of God's love for those who are his own.

As it has been said, If we earnestly seek God, we have already been found by him.

I can only conceive of the universe as a thought in the mind of God.

Baker, Mathematician

EIGHT

WHICH IS CORRECT, CREATION OR EVOLUTION?

There is an old joke that goes, Where does an 800 lb. gorilla sit when he enters your living room? The answer is, Any where he wants to. Likewise, when you become convinced of the existence of God, then the question of how he created becomes just a matter of curiosity. It really does not make that much difference then. God can do it any which way he wants to. The new, controversial explanation is the theory of evolution. To take a strictly secular view of that process assumes an astoundingly, miraculous event of spontaneous, complex happenstance that simply boggles the mind, and is illogical.

In the second option there is the special creation of mankind in a world that evolved: the evidence of evolution regarding mankind was inserted in order to give some order for the sake of scientific development. Of course there can be other motives for that view, such as an aversion to being "a monkey's uncle." Whatever the case, a God capable of creating the universe is certainly capable of creating it any which way he so chooses.

The third option is creation in six (24 hour) days, in strict, literal adherence to the description given in Scripture, and with a history built into it for the sake of advancement by science. But once you accept the fact that God created this material world, then it doesn't seem to make any difference how. God can create any which way he chooses.

What really seems to be at stake is the literal inerrancy of the Bible, free of error, letter by letter, word by word. That view of the Bible, both Old and New Testaments, is logically indefensible, simply because we do not have the original manuscripts. But we seem to be mighty close to the original form, even with the understanding that the copying of manuscripts are attributed to one scribe or another depending on the type of error he typically made. To show how difficult the formation of a reliable composite text is, the oldest manuscript I have seen a photograph of was written in Greek, all in capital letters (apparently out of respect), on vellum, with no punctuation, and with no spacing between words and sentences. The text was one solid block of capital letters, consequently you had to know what it said before you could read it. But I believe we are so close to the original in the accepted composite text that every detail in every account is reliably accurate. Saying all of that makes the accepted Greek text all the more believable, and rightfully the rule of faith, and canon for the church.

The book of Genesis, in the third chapter, contains the account of Adam and Eve in the idyllic Garden of Eden, their disobedience, and their punishment for sin, which included a curse upon the land so that it would be physically hard to gain a living from it. That factor was a kind of twist put into the creation when they were expelled from

Eden because of their sin. At the other end of the Bible, Saint John in his Revelation tells that God will make it like it was, like it was supposed to be, as in the Garden of Eden. He will not be defeated by human sin; he will triumph with a recreated heaven and earth, just like Eden.

In the Letter to the Romans Saint Paul makes the following statement which many people regard as literary hyperbole, but I am convinced that it is true and a result of his legitimate religious experiences, for it agrees with the experiences of other Christian mystics.

> We know that the whole creation has been groaning as in the pains of childbirth right up to the present time. Not only so, but we ourselves, who have the firstfruits of the Spirit, groan inwardly as we wait eagerly for our adoption as sons, the redemption of our bodies. For in this hope we were saved. But hope that is seen is no hope at all. Who hopes for what he already has? But if we hope for what we do not yet have, we wait for it patiently.
>
> (Romans 8:22-25)

In his life on earth, Jesus showed great compassion for all life, and especially for children. That is not surprising considering that he is the one through whom God created the world we see about us. Scripture claims the resurrected, victorious Lord Christ is enthroned at the right hand of God the Father Almighty, and rules both heaven and earth. This is the one with whom we express solidarity when we pray in Jesus' name. When you stop and think about it, it really is an extraordinary thing.

There is another red flag, so to speak, that is run up the flagpole when creation by God is considered. What about natural evil? If what is constructive of life is considered good, and what is destructive of life is evil, then all of the destructive forces in nature fall into the category of natural evil. In this category are such things as hurricanes, tornados, and the origin of diseases. There are three possibilities, and no matter how a person waltzes around the subject, it still comes down to these three. First, God was unable to create the material world without natural evil in it. Then by definition he is not almighty. And by the way, what else can he not do? We are in jeopardy if this is the case, and it is no game.

Second, God deliberately created the world with natural evil (as it characteristically is termed) in it. Then that would indicate an evil side to God, something not to be taken lightly. And we are in deep, deep trouble. Waist deep in the big muddy.

Third, natural evil finds its origin elsewhere, not in God, but in Satan, whom Jesus referred to as the "Prince of this world" (John 14:30) – the world of people (according to the Greek word used for world) who live and love in opposition to the will of God. They are rebel subjects, but subjects nevertheless. No matter how much we balk at the idea of such a force of evil loose in this world today, from cover to cover in the Bible, natural evil is laid at Satan's doorstep. When in the righteous judgment of God for punishment, or for the potentially redemptive effect of trouble or suffering when properly borne, God needs only to withdraw some measure of his protection. (cf. Job; Luke 22:31-34)

As the future rolls into the present, we are mindful that St. Paul wrote, "For the world in its present form is passing away." (I Corinthians 7:31b) From the perspective of the 21st century, we can vouch for that from experience. And as it passes, the future – that land known only to God, and those to whom he chooses to reveal it – relentlessly comes to us, and we find that we really are "pilgrims and strangers" in a world shot through with chaos and turbulence, those enigmas of modern science, and ourselves hapless but hopeful, called to be combatants in a cosmic struggle between good and evil. We are hardly bereft of challenges, and we each find our destiny here and in eternity,

And perhaps along the way, to see a world in a grain of sand, and a heaven in a wild flower, hold infinity in the palm of your hand, and eternity in an hour.
by William Blake

*We hold these Truths to be self-evident, that all Men are cre-
ated equal, that they are endowed by their Creator with certain unalienable Rights, that among these are Life, Liberty,
and the Pursuit of Happiness.*

The Declaration of Independence

NINE

HOW ARE PEOPLE EQUAL?

Exactly how are people created equal so that they are
given certain inherent, irrevocable rights by God, apparently as a consequence of being human? There are some
observable ways in which they are not equal: physically –
people vary widely in height, weight, color of skin, hair,
eyes, and health – even in vulnerability to numerous diseases which varies immensely from person to person. In
mental ability people vary all over the I.Q. scale, which is a
factor that education officials and politicians have not yet
comprehended or are not courageous enough to bring up.

But that still leaves us with the question, How are
people equal? The answer I propose is that all people are
equal in worth in the sight of God. That then becomes
mandatory as the base line of worth that obligates every
society to provide equality of treatment in civil, political,
and legal rights for all people within its borders, and not just

the legal citizens. Such socially imposed designations as citizenship do not modify God's guarantee of worth for each individual. As far as cognitive ability is concerned, it has absolutely no bearing on human, civil, or political rights. If it did, we would all be in trouble, for there is always someone that is smarter than our self.

As it is, our being created equal refers to being created in the Imago Deo, in the Image of God, that is to say, being able to turn the mind back upon itself in moral self reflection. That is just one step ahead of many animals who are able to reason and solve problems, and some even make crude tools. With mankind's genetic heritage there is a very thin difference between us and the higher animals. The distinction of being able to turn the mind back upon itself in moral self reflection was made by Pierre Teilhard de Chardin. That commonality that we all have gives us each equality of worth before both God and man. Plus, we have the rightful potential destiny of being a true son or daughter of God by choice, for we were created for that fellowship with God, which is an incredible opportunity. That enhanced bond with God is something, I think, that is only rarely attained to any real significant degree, because it takes a regimen of meditative prayer and an openness of spirit to greater comprehension of God.

In reference to equality of people, preferential treatment to one group violates the equality principle stated in the Declaration of Independence. It demeans the others.

As far as "Unalienable Rights" are concerned, government owes its citizens protection not just from enemies from within and without its borders, but also from environmentally destructive actions of private enterprise and agencies that shorten our life.

In regard to liberty, freedom is never absolute. As the old example goes, you are not free to falsely yell "fire" in a crowded theater. There is a principle in sociology that the more densely populated an area is, the less personal freedom each individual has. For instance, a person who lives on a farm can safely do target practice with a rifle in his back yard, but not a person who lives in a city. Freedom always has been a relative thing, and it is different things to different people.

Likewise, "pursuit of happiness" must have limitations, because happiness is different things to different people. At the extreme, in some people it is murderous. Individually, pursuit of happiness commonly is a relative thing – relative to the social norm of behavior, which determines its acceptability under human law. As opposed to the leveling down of popular morality, all in the name and guise of freedom, there is a moral grain to the universe, the will of God, that we violate at our peril. One conspicuous violation is infant sacrifice, abortion, all in the name of freedom, a very selfish twisting of the concept of freedom. As it is said, "You don't break the Ten Commandments; you only break yourself upon them."

The bright spot in all of this is that so far America has always escaped the forces of destruction. Let us pray God's mercy, blessing, and protection – now and always.

You know the old Caledonia Railway Station, one cold east windy morning I met Satan there.

Robert Louis Stevenson

TEN

DOES DUALITY (GOOD AND EVIL) EXTEND INTO THE REALM OF THE SPIRIT?

In this world shot through with duality – good and evil, hot and cold, positive and negative, light and dark, up and down – it would greatly surprise me if both good and evil were not in the realm of the spirit, which is another dimension of reality. But the experience of Robert Louis Stevenson is so alien to what most of us have experienced that the tendency is to dismiss his account as not valid. However, it certainly is invalid to make our own religious experience, or lack of it, the rule for all people in all times and in all places. Therefore, we need to take a careful look at the subject.

First, the existence of Satan – an active, personal force of evil at loose in this world – is affirmed from cover to cover in the Bible, in both the Old Testament and the New. Jesus referred to him also as the "Prince of this world" (John12:31; 14:30; 16:11) – that is to say, the world of people who live and love in opposition to the will of God, and that seems to include a lot.

55

Of course when one thinks on this subject, it brings to mind the movie, *The Exorcist*. Everybody knows that the movie was based on a novel; however, the book was based on a real life account. In the late 1940's the report came to the attention of a Washington newspaper editor that a young boy, about twelve years old as I recall, had undergone the exorcism of a demon. A reporter was sent by the editor to verify the story. When he came back he wanted to write a lengthy account of the story, but the editor told him that was one of the subjects you don't write about; instead he was to submit just a brief announcement of it. He followed orders, but later wrote and published the book.

At the St. Meinrad Archabbey library I read the real summary account of what happened.   Apparently after exhibiting paranormal phenomenon associated with him, and being tested for physical and mental disorders (of which he showed none), he had been taken to a hospital in the St. Louis, Missouri area.   There, while strapped to a gurney, large scratches appeared on his body. Welts could perhaps be explained away by the mind's ability to vary the temperature of the hands by as much as $10°$ F either direction, but scratches could not be explained away because his hands were restrained. Added to that, he was speaking curses in ancient languages that he had no way of knowing. The priest who was to perform the exorcism did a thirty day black fast before he started the ritual. When the name of the demon was demanded, its name was one mentioned in the Bible. It was successfully exorcised. This case is very persuasive.

Adolf Hitler, as a young man, spent one night in a park atop a small mountain, and had what amounted to a religious experience in which he tapped into the evil side of the realm of the spirit. He reportedly had an extraordinary experience that gave him the sense of destiny of "Fuhrer" (leader) of the German people; the rest is history. If what is real is what is, then he probably was the most capable leader of the twentieth century; it is just that he led in the wrong direction. He was a brilliant, cunning dictator, a fiery orator very much in touch with the soul of the German people. But he was a totally ruthless, corrupt man who came to power.

Near the beginning of his road of conquest, when he proposed conquering Czechoslovakia, his general staff said it couldn't be done. Hitler arranged a meeting with the president of Czechoslovakia at the Chancellery on March 14, 1939, and brow beat him into surrendering the country; he took the country without a shot being fired. From then on the general staff deferred to his judgment; he seemed to be able to do the impossible. He evidently was a magnetic leader, after all, in the last hours of Berlin it was the Spanish Blue Division that provided the primary defense of the city. But throughout his dictatorship, the Allied leaders consistently under estimated him, and dismissed him as just a rabble rouser.   On the morning of September 28, 1938, the French Ambassador, Andre Francois-Poncet, met with Hitler in the chancellery and warned him that,

> You deceive yourself, Chancellor, if you believe you can confine the conflict to Czechoslovakia. If you attack that country, you will set all Europe ablaze.

> (Payne, Robert. The Life and Death of Adolf Hitler. New York: Praeger Pub., 1973. p.326)

He subsequently did that for the sake of personal ambition. It has been estimated that forty million people died as a result of World War II. This utterly evil man who emerged out of nowhere, initiator of death camps and the Holocaust, caused incalculable suffering, death, and destruction. This man, who dominated the twentieth century, left an imprint on history that will persist for centuries to come.

Adolf Hitler simply cannot be dismissed as mentally ill because naming something does not explain it. His record of evil is simply off the charts, and yet he came up from nothing and evidently was destitute for several years as a young man. Nobody that effectively evil does it alone; he undoubtedly had the inside help of Satan, the Prince of this world. He simply must have been possessed, and if not, then we are in far, far deeper trouble than we can possibly imagine. As it is, the cosmic conflict between good and evil is deadly serious. And remember, in the Greek language of the New Testament when demonic possession is mentioned, it means exactly what it says. There was a separate term used for mental illness: "he is beside himself."

There was a very interesting case in Russia during the time of World War I. It is that of Rasputin, the wandering spiritual adviser, a staret as they are termed in the Eastern Orthodox Church. He dominated the Czarina while the Czar was away leading the war effort. But he was utterly corrupt, and was having an extremely destructive effect on the government of Russia, and consequently probably made it vulnerable to the Communist Revolution. A few noblemen decided that it was expedient that Rasputin be killed. They invited him to a villa with the promise of food, drink, and women. They fed him enough poison to kill twenty men but there was no visible effect, and he began to demand the promised women. One nobleman then came down the stairway with a revolver and emptied it into him at point blank range. Rasputin still was able to break through some French doors into the garden, where they brought him down with a steel poker. They wrapped his body in chains, with padlocks, and dumped him in the Neva River. Even though it was winter time, when his body washed ashore three days later, he had worked himself half way out of his chains.

One of the noblemen who participated in the killing of Rasputin was interviewed (during the late 1990's, as I recall) in Paris where he lived and subsequently died. He said of Rasputin, "It was like trying to kill the Devil himself! He wouldn't die!" It is accounts like that which confirm the biblical witness that (like it or not, recognize it or not) we are involved in a cosmic conflict between good and evil that extends into both the material and spiritual dimensions of reality. It is terribly serious, as is shown by the history of mankind written in blood. As Abraham I. Heschel wrote,

> The absence of the awareness of the mystery of evil is a tragic blindness of modern man. In his vocabulary the word is missing. But without an awareness of sin, without the fear of evil, there can be no repentance.

> ("A Hebrew Evaluation of Reinhold Niebuhr" Reinhold Niebuhr. Volume II. The Macmillan Co.: New York, 1956. p.395)

In the Bible the subversion of the forces of nature to cause the events which we class as natural evil, is nearly always laid at the doorstep of Satan. In the story of Job, God only needed to withdraw his protection a specific amount to allow trouble to come from Satan who subverted the forces of nature, and evidently is the source of nature being "red in tooth and claw."

It is interesting that in the accounts of the Temptation of Jesus by Satan (Matthew 4:1-11; Mark 1:12-13; Luke 4:1-13), they read like a rabbinic disputation, with the two countering each other with scriptural quotations. The calm courtesy of the interchange seems to give validity to the claim in the Apocrypha that Satan, a fallen archangel, who originally was sort of a prosecuting attorney of mankind, fell from grace for the same reason that mankind did – pride, the inordinate love of self more than God and more than other people. Therefore pride is the arrogating of self to try to be god of one's own life. Consequently it is rebellion against God. But despite that, because of the rank Satan held, there is a certain courtesy extended, perhaps also because he is now "Prince of this world" – the world of people who live and love against God's will. They are God's rebel subjects, but subjects nevertheless.

Before leaving the subject of the Temptation of Jesus in the Wilderness, note that the first two temptations are to verify that he really is uniquely the Son of God. They are like saying, "Check it out, Jesus." The third temptation is to switch sides, and gain "all the kingdoms of the world and their splendor." Being Messiah was a heavy power trip, but here was a shortcut to power. But he turned down all three temptations, and after his ascension God made him ruler of both heaven and earth.

There is a popular allegorical interpretation that the first two are temptations to gain adherents by providing the multitudes food and miracles, and he passes the test on all three then. However, he later feeds several multitudes, and performs a number of public miracles; this brings his score down to 33%, which is failing in anybody's grade book. This shows that some scriptural interpretations are not adequately thought out.

There is a military acronym, RHIP, which stands for "rank has its privileges" that sort of helps explain a relevant passage from the Letter of Jude in the New Testament. Jude apparently was a half brother of Jesus, which is a subject in itself. In his letter addressed to Christians in general, he cites the account in the Apocrypha of the burial of Moses' body.

> In the very same way, these dreamers pollute their own bodies, reject authority and slander celestial beings. But even the archangel Michael, when he was disputing with the devil about the body of Moses, did   not dare to bring a slanderous accusation against him, but said, "The Lord rebuke you!" Yet these men speak abusively against whatever they do not understand; and what things they do understand by instinct, like unreasoning animals – these are the very things that destroy them.
>
> (Jude 8-12)

The details of evil in that unseen realm of the spirit generally remain an enigma to us, but it is one of the perils of life.

William James sarcastically noted:

In the Louvre there is a picture by Guido Reni, of St. Michael with his foot on Satan's neck. The richness of the picture is in large part due to the fiend's figure being there. The richness of its allegorical meaning also is due to his being there – that is, the world is all the richer for having a devil in it, so long as we keep our foot upon his neck.

(William James. <u>The Varieties of Religious Experience.</u> New York: The New American Library of World Literature, Inc. 1958. p55)

ELEVEN

WHY IS THERE A POPULAR FASCINATION WITH EVIL?

It all goes back to the Garden of Eden, and the temptation based on pride – the one basis for all sin. Pride, as the word is used in the Christian faith, is the inordinate love of self, more than God and more than others. And the serpent, Satan, subtly hooked Eve into disobeying God, for he assured her that, "Your eyes will be opened, and you will be like God, knowing good and evil," (Genesis 3:5b) – to experience evil firsthand, to know it experientially. The temptation was to arrogate herself to the level of God, to be god of her own life. To be free! Free at last! Free to live and love in opposition to God's will. Perhaps there always is a degree of selfishness in freedom. After all, all of our mitzvahs (religious good deeds) are flawed in motive. And you never in this earthly phase of life achieve absolute freedom; there are always some social or legal limitations that we function under.

There are essentially three forms of pride: Spiritual pride, pride of knowledge, and pride of position – position as a result of money or power of office or function. If the truth were known, all three of those forms of pride are routes to power, and generally are a revolt against God. There is quite a bit of that going around.

There is an old saying that "those who fail to learn from the past, are doomed to repeat it." In the past, interest in religion was cyclic. But something new has been added to the mix of factors, and it is television, personal computers, and motion pictures with hi-tech special effects. It all makes for extremely effective packaging for perversions ranging from violence and promiscuous sexual behavior all the way to thrill-killings, which are a form of sexual deviation, to infant sacrifice in abortion, so that the female will not have to say no. The legislatures and courts have shown a remarkable dedication to exaggerate the value of sexual climax. But, what goes around, comes around, and we have seen the results of the cheapening of regard for human life – in the discarding in the trash of live human infants, in the increasing frequency of kidnapping and murder of children, and in "euthanasia" in the execution by starvation of a conscious, innocent woman by the state of Florida and its court system, because they didn't think her life was worth living. Just wait until that factor plays itself out in our culture. We are all put in jeopardy by it.

An Episcopalian priest told me of a church member who had been crippled since early childhood. One day the priest received a telephone call that the man had a heart attack, and was in the hospital. The priest said he dreaded the hospital visit to see the man, for he could well imagine the tale of woe and sorrow he would be obligated to hear. When he arrived there, he was surprised to hear him say, "I've had a good life!"

All of life is lived under the eyes of God – God who acts in history. From cover to cover in the Bible it speaks of God's love for mankind, but on appropriate occasions he acts in righteous anger, and he can be heavy-handed, as witnessed by the judgment that fell upon Sodom and Gomorrah. In that story,

> In the statement with which Yahweh takes Abraham into his confidence he speaks quite openly as the protector of justice in all lands. ... Yahweh has received great complaints about Sodom and Gomorrah. The word, "outcry", is a technical legal term and designates the cry for help which one who suffers a great injustice screams. (We even know what the cry was, namely, "Foul play!" [translation of the Hebrew word] hamas, Jer. 20:28; Hab.1:2; Job 19:7) With this cry for help (which corresponds to the old German "Zeterruf"), he appeals for the protection of the legal community. What it does not hear or grant, however, comes directly before Yahweh as the guardian of all right. (cf. Gen. 4:10)
> (Rad, Gerhard Von. <u>Genesis</u>.
> Philadelphia: Westminister
> Press, 1972. pp. 210-211)

Remember also, when Jesus saw Jerusalem from the top of the Mount of Olives during the Triumphal Entry, he prophesied the destruction that would come upon the city, "because you did not recognize the time of God's coming to you." (Luke 19:44c) That used to be referred to as "the iron in the Gospel."

One thing is for sure, the entertainment industry knows exactly what they are doing, and that includes Hollywood. They not only are trying to meet a market, but I think they also seem to be successfully trying to generate a market – in evil as entertainment, hence all of the movies and television programs on witchcraft, Satanism, and other forms of the occult. I suspect that the saying applies, "Payday someday."

In the last half of the movie, "Apocalypse Now," there was a curious comment about the Colonel, who was one of the two major characters in the story. A person said of the Colonel,

> He isn't insane; his mind is sane.
> It is his soul that is mad ...
> It isn't a matter of insanity but of evil.

That's a rather interesting observation, considering it was a secularly produced motion picture. But in this case art mimics reality – with its daily stories of perversion and violence.

The two Greek words in the Gospel accounts that are transliterated soul and spirit each have the meaning of "thinking, willing, feeling." Consequently they each are about equal to our modern word, "personality." Therefore, "soul" and "spirit" have very relevant meanings today. Both words are used interchangeably in the Gospel accounts.

The curious thing about the words "soul" and "spirit" is that in comparison with the modern word "personality", there is one significant difference – the soul/spirit has an enduring quality that lives on eternally. It is one aspect that extends beyond what we normally associate with the concept of personality. Therefore, since the personality lives on eternally, it is very important the kind of person you are in the process of becoming. And it has ramifications for what we call emotional or mental illness.

There are more things in heaven and earth, Horatio, than are dreamt of in your philosophy.

from "Hamlet" I, 66

TWELVE

IS THERE ANY REALITY TO RELIGIOUS EXPERIENCE?

Religious experience, as I use the term, is a phenomenal (out of the ordinary) experience related to a person's religious beliefs. It therefore covers a wide range of experiences, as William James noted in his book The Varieties of Religious Experience. In addition, I think that what a person is able to experience in the area of paranormal religious experience is limited by two factors: the will of God, and the person's horizon of religious expectation - the outer limit of the person's belief in what is possible for God to do in this world.

It should be noted that all prayer, even just a simple prayer of thanksgiving, is dependent on the principle that God acts in this time, and in this world, in a material way. Otherwise prayer would be pointless if we thanked him for what he hadn't done, or asked him for what he was unable or unwilling to do. However, we have the good fortune that God is almighty, and his attitude towards us is love. Therefore, prayer is efficacious, and God does answer in accordance with his will, which apparently is the best for all concerned in the perspective of eternity. By the way, the Greek word, agape, that is translated as "love" in the New Testament (regarding God's love for us, and our love for God and others) is defined as "unwilling to do without", and therefore is a will-centered response, capable of being commanded by Jesus. Unfortunately, our word "love" includes the meanings of the four separately named different kinds of love in the Greek language. Consequently, men tend to have an aversion to the major ethical theme of love in Christianity until they become familiar with the difference in the languages, and realize the faith is not effeminate.

Experience indicates that the realm of the Spirit is the primary, or most elemental reality, over which this material world is just a veneer. The realm of the spirit is a different dimension of reality. And time is poetically the context in which events happen. Philosophically it is the sequentiality of events, the one-after-anotherness of events. Scientifically time is a ratio of mass and speed, and therefore a very this-worldly thing. In the realm of the spirit there apparently is a form of sequentiality, but of a different nature than earth-time. Time gives an irreversibility to the actions of our will, and materiality gives a concreteness, a reality imprint to the actions of our will. Time and materiality together give a once-for-allness to our actions, a personal trace in history, and therefore an ethical responsibility. As one writer put it, "Man does not die in a ditch like a dog, but at home in history."

The following examples of religious experiences are all from the present generation. One religious experience reported was a quiet and very intense perception of the unity with all creation (even the trees), and accompanied by a phe-nomenal sense of timelessness. As reported, that event was calmly rational, and the most truly alive and accurate per-ception of reality that the person experienced in all of his life, and it was accompanied by a pervasive and gentle sense of bondedness with all creation, and a consequent sense of God's love and presence - one who fills all of heaven and earth. It was a validating and transforming experience, with a sense of belongingness.

I think that, in a manner of speaking, a person must "pay his dues." That is to say, there must be a seriousness and consistency to the person's religious quest as a Christian before God grants the grace of a faith confirming religious experience. Remember what an angel said to the prophet Daniel:

> Do not be afraid, Daniel. Since the first day that you set your mind to gain understanding and to humble yourself before your God, your words were heard, and I have come in response to them.
> (Daniel 10:12)

As different as individuals are, both in experience and genet-ic endowment, it is not surprising that God grants a variety of religious experiences. And it is absurd for one person to assume that his or her own religious experience (or lack of it) is the rule for all people in all places, and in all times.

One lady told me of an incident that happened just after she had gone to bed, and had not yet gone to sleep. Jesus came in through the bedroom door and stood at the foot of the bed. I asked how he was dressed. "Did he wear a modern business suit and shoes?" "No," she said. "He wore a robe." She didn't see his feet. I asked what he said, and she told me, "He didn't say anything. He just stood there for a minute, and then turned and left." The next morning she got word that her fiancé had been killed in an accident.

I think that because of her genuinely devout life of faith, she was given advance consolation to prepare her for the grievous news that would come in the morning. In allusion to a modern gospel song, she had "one more hill to climb." The story is an example of Jesus' love for one of his adopted sisters in the faith. She could honestly say, "I have learned to trust in Jesus, through it all."

Another story that involved an extraordinary experience was told to me by a lady, who had two female cousins, one of them noted for her prophetic gift. The three of them, in their middle teenage years, were in the dining room of the house when suddenly the prophetically gifted girl said, "Look!" as she pointed into the living room to their grandfather who was seated in a chair by the wall, underneath a picture of Jesus knocking at the door. But the picture had changed. All three girls saw it showing Jesus turned towards their grandfather with his arms invitingly extended. Their grandfather died suddenly a few days later. Evidently he had received the call home from the Lord Christ.

Along a different vein, Dr. Herman Norton, a professor of American church history at the Divinity School of Vanderbilt University, made a study of the so-called "snake-handling" churches of the Appalachian Mountain region. He found that they did not handle poisonous snakes in order to prove the adequacy of their faith, but did it because they interpreted the verse Mark 16:18a as commanding it. Whatever the case, he said he attended one meeting where halfway through the service a large cardboard box full of poisonous snakes was dumped out on the floor while the people were up out of their seats and moving around, with hands lifted up and waving, and their faces all looking up praising God. Yet nobody was bitten by a snake despite all of the intermingling, motion, and sound. I think the moral of that story is that God takes care of his own even when they err slightly in reading the Bible.

A more incredible story was an article that appeared in a major newspaper in about 1975; as I recall it was an Associated Press news release. The story was of a boy about eight years old who lived in North Carolina; he came down the hall of the house one evening to the living room where his parents were entertaining guests, and told his parents and the others that he could see out of his bad eye. The interesting thing was that his right eye had been amputated two years previously. When they checked they found that he really could see out of his glass eye.

It turned out that he and been praying to God to heal his "bad eye" without realizing that what he was asking was absolutely impossible, but God refused to turn down the fervent request of this young boy who asked in humble faith.

The local newspaper ran the story, and it was picked up by the news service who sent a reporter and a cameraman to investigate. They first stopped at the ophthalmologist's office to find out whether or not one of his eyes had been amputated, and if so which one. The doctor confirmed that he had amputated the right eye due to an injury.

They then went out to the family's house and introduced themselves and asked if they could test the boy's vision in his right eye. They bandaged over his left eye so that he could not possibly see out of it. In order to prevent him from reading something that he had already memorized, they gave him their film package to read, and he read it. They thought perhaps the glass eye was focusing light on the stub of the optic nerve, therefore they asked his parents to remove the glass eye, and when they did he could see out of the empty eye socket. The reporter and cameraman decided it was a case of extra sensory perception (ESP) which simply means "we don't know," and they referred him to the ESP laboratory at Duke University. [Now it is separate and known as the Rhine Research Center, located in Durham, North Carolina.]

But remember, naming something does not explain it. For instance naming a disease by giving a name to a cluster of symptoms does not explain the origin of the disease or why the person contracted it. In a different field of learning, remember that naming gravity, and even quantifying it, did not explain it. It was the last half of the 20th century before a good popular explanation could be given to gravity that would begin to be logical. Naming something simply does not explain it.

I don't think that God will grant you a religious experience that will exceed your horizon of religious expectations, or your sense of the limits of reality.

I have a friend (let's call him Jim) who was a combat fighter pilot in Vietnam. He is one of the most normal individuals that I have ever known. During his stint of duty there he flew ground support in an A-1 Skyraider. It was a propeller driven airplane, with a 3,000 horsepower radial reciprocating (piston) engine. The airplane was fitted with enough armaments to give it more striking power than a World War II B-17. Since the A-1 was designed in the 1940's it did not have an ejection seat, but was retrofitted with a rocket powered escaped system, called the "Yankee seat."

One day, on what turned out to be his last combat mission, Jim was providing fighter escort for a helicopter borne assault force, when his A-1 was hit by ground fire, began burning, and went out of control. As the situation increased in intensity, and as the airplane spun toward the ground, he felt an added Presence. He ejected, and soon came down into some trees on a hillside. The Presence he had sensed became as a bright light, with form and substance, watching over the life or death drama occurring there. At this point he saw four soldiers from different eras: a Roman Legionnaire; a World War I "doughboy"; and two others from different times and nations. One of them said, "Now you are one of us." Then they faded.

This was not a dream, nor did he at any time lose consciousness. He was totally alert and conscious, monitoring everything that was happening around him in the material dimension of reality. For instance, he saw the huge ball of flame as the airplane exploded against the hillside, while at the same time losing his helmet as he crashed into a tree. Activating his emergency radio, he told his friends he was alive, but needed help. "Right arm paralyzed, apparently broken, otherwise OK, tangled in chute harness, having trouble getting free with only one hand."

Then he prayed, "Lord, my function of protecting the ground troops is ended. I'll be outnumbered and outgunned. Do I fight or surrender?"

The answer came back, "You are a soldier – you fight as long as you are able." … Jim responded, "Lord, I am not afraid of death. But I am afraid of the process, especially here where I know what these people do to Americans that come into their hands." The rresponse was, "You will be alright. I will hold your hand."

"OK. But if it wouldn't upset some great plan of yours, you know I've got four little girls back home, and I sure would like to be there to see them grow up." "OK, but that won't be so easy."

In just a moment the answer came over the radio that he shouldn't shoot if he saw somebody coming up the hillside. To protect him until a rescue helicopter retrieved him, some troops had been landed farther down the hillside. The copilot of the first helicopter had been lowered by cable, and helped Jim get disentangled from the parachute harness and shrouds, and onto the seat of the tree penetrater, which lifted him up and out.

He later wondered what the statement meant, "That won't be so easy." As it turned out, he saw two of his four daughters get divorced, his wife die of cancer, and his youngest daughter was killed in an automobile crash. I think that was the difficulty referred to.

With the modern concept of the world about us, cosmology, a person cannot logically, categorically dismiss such stories by use of an imported theology, alien to both Christianity and modern science.

My words fly up, my thoughts remain below:
Words without thoughts never to heaven go.

Hamlet, III

THIRTEEN

WHY PRAY? IS THERE ANYTHING TO PRAYER BESIDES POSITIVE THINKING?

Probably more has been written about prayer, with less said, than any other subject in the field of religion. Most of what is written seems to be about the feelings of prayer, rather than specific information. And there are people who pray with about the same confidence as wishing upon a star, and there are others who pray just in case there's anything to it. Of course there are those who pray with real sincerity, and sometimes even in desperation, as the case from colonial times of one man who wrote in his diary,

Between the saddle and the ground,
Mercy I asked, and mercy I found.

I remember Professor James Glasse came into class at seminary one day and announced, "I don't believe in the power of prayer!" That got everybody's attention, and after a brief pause he continued, "But I do believe in the power of God! We have no power over him to manipulate him." Properly

76

stated, prayer is efficacious; it is of beneficial effect. It directly approaches what mankind was created for, which is fellowship with God.

When you consider how God answers prayer, there are three stock answers: yes, no, and wait. Most of us have lived long enough to be grateful to God that some of our prayers were not answered. I remember one lay elder in the church who when he retired he very much needed a part time job to supplement his retirement income. He applied for a job at a government facility, and prayed hard for it, but he was passed over and turned down. Then a remarkable thing happened; he got a far superior job with the city that was a real joy to him, and paid significantly more money than the other one did. The way it all turned out, God had something better in mind for him than what he was praying for. That was why he got a "no" from God on that. It is another example of God's love for those who are truly his own.

There is one passage that is often quoted regarding prayer; when Jesus told his disciples that he would soon be going to be with the Father, God in heaven, he said:

> I will do whatever you ask in my name, so the Son may bring glory to the Father. You may ask me for anything and I will do it.
>
> (John 14:13-14)

In all probability that promise was directed only to the inner Twelve Disciples, otherwise it just doesn't necessarily always work out that way. One basic principle is that you don't hang a whole theology on one verse. Instead you decide its meaning in the light of, and as part of, the totality of the New Testament Scriptures, one unified body of truth. Also, according to Hans von Campenhausen, in his book, The Formation of the Christian Bible, the writings that were left out of the New Testament were properly excluded, and those that were included in the canon, properly belong there.

On another occasion, apparently including more disciples than just the Twelve, Jesus said,

> Again, I tell you that if two of you on earth agree about anything you ask for, it will be done for you by my Father in heaven. For where two or three come together in my name, there am I with them.

> (Matthew 18:19-20)

If that was a hard and fast rule, rigidly applied, there would be a sinfully large number of Christian couples who would have won the lottery. But there is at least one thing that trumps the statement, the will of God. As St. John records for believers,

> This is the assurance we have in approaching God: that if we ask anything according to his will, he hears us. And if we know that he hears us – whatever we ask – we know that we have what we asked of him.

> (I John 1:13-14)

Experience indicates that in answering prayer, God seems to operate on the principle of what is the best for all concerned in the perspective of eternity. That, then, is the will of God.

One lesson from all that has been stated above is that Jesus could not state in one sentence all there is to say about prayer. That is why there is a little bit here and there throughout his time of teaching.

There remains the very interesting point that Jesus advised his followers when they prayed to do it in his name. It evidently was not a rigid rule, for the model prayer he taught them – the Lord's Prayer – does not close with that. And it is not a magical incantation. St. Paul reveals the reason for the practice: It expresses a unity, a solidarity with Jesus, the Lord Christ. Because the name of a person represents that person, there seems to be a spiritual bond that merges the two. Therefore invoking the name of Jesus establishes a linkage, a bond, and consequently the claim of being one of God's own, in the family of God, an adopted brother or sister of Christ by right of baptism. Consequently, since it claims a solidarity with Christ in the dimension of the spirit, it is a defense against the presence or the assault by evil. And every worship service in a church or synagogue is in essence a prayer to God.

Jakob Bohme (1575 to 1624) was a Christian mystic who said that if a person could totally focus his will in prayer, miracles would happen. Discursive prayer (using words silently or orally) seems to be more effective when preceded by a period of meditation. Meditation is a means of quieting and focusing the mind and will, and consequently relaxing. Usually at least ten minutes is spent in meditation before beginning the prayer.

As the saying goes, to pray without thanksgiving is to clip the wings of prayer. Besides, God, who knows the hearts and minds of each of us, already knows what we need. Therefore, the more we progress in the faith, evidently the more prayer reduces to thanksgiving.

Bach gave us God's word,
Mozart gave us God's laughter,
Beethoven gave us God's fire,
God gave us music that we might
pray without words
                  from a German opera house.

FOURTEEN

WHAT IS THE PURPOSE AND USE OF MEDITATION?

As stated before, the process of meditation is to focus both mind and will to where there is a clarity of thought. As it has been said, the mind is like a wild horse going off in all directions at once. Meditation is a process to focus the mind and will that includes several dozen techniques. The most simple one is breath counting. That can be done by silently counting one on the inhale, and two on the exhale, and repeating that sequence silently for preferably at least ten minutes. Meditation also can be done by counting breaths sequentially – up to four breaths for Caucasians, and seven breaths for Asians – counting just on the inhale, or just on the exhale, up to the number four, or seven. Those two are the most neutral forms of meditation.

There is another form of meditation where you silently read hymns that are addressed to God, whereas gospel songs are not typically addressed to God, but are a celebration of the faith.

Another form of meditation, among many forms, is one that I highly recommend; it is the Jesus Prayer. The full form of it is,

> Lord Jesus Christ, Son of God
> have mercy on me a sinner.

Some people object to the last phrase and leave off the words "a sinner." Using the Jesus Prayer in such repetition has been said to help significantly in converting the subconscious.

The ones who regularly practice meditation claim that it will have a calming effect on both pulse rate and blood pressure. If a person using the breath counting method experiences the effect of increasing the breathing rate, then it should be discontinued. Also, if the person is spiritually open to it, there may be one of the more spectacular gifts of the Spirit, such as the ones listed in I Corinthians 12. One seminary classmate in a course on prayer experienced an occurrence of clairvoyance, like that in the calling of Nathanael. (John 1:43-51)

There is a style of music called "cosmic blues," or "waking up in the middle of the night blues." It refers to the situation at one time or another in many people's life when so many things have gone wrong that a sense of gloom and doom sets in. In the extreme form of it there may be a sense of being God-forsaken. Another term for it is "the dark night of the soul." It is a time when all things seem to have gone wrong, and there's nothing left to go on except faith itself. It is the true test of faith, and, as Robert Browning puts it, we stumble at truth's greatest test.

When we are young there tends to be a great appreciation for the beauty of the created world around us, especially the heavens above. As the years go by, if the person allows it to happen, then the challenges of life take their toll. As Aldous Huxley admitted, in later life he now looked at the heavens in the same way he looked upon the faded wallpaper in a railway waiting station. There is a way to solve this condition; it is called "the Blessing of the Memories;" it is really a very simple process. You think back as far as you can remember to your earliest memory, and you thank God for that event in your life. Then you progress forward in life, thanking God for each event and thing you can remember, both the good and the bad – not for the bad itself, but for the good that came in spite of the bad. This process can take a while to do it properly. It can take anywhere from a full day to a full week, depending on how thoroughly it is done.

One thing should be pointed out, this should be done at every major turning point in life, especially in every major decision, and in every period of the dark night of the soul. It enables you to come to terms with God, with yourself, and with life as you know it. It has the added advantage that it brings the blessing of God on you, because you're thereby reconciled to him.

The absence of the awareness of the mystery of evil is a tragic blindness of modern man. In his vocabulary the word is missing. But without an awareness of sin, without the fear of evil, there can be no repentance.

(Abraham I. Heschel. "A Hebrew Evaluation of Reinhold Niebuhr" Reinhold Niebuhr: His Religious, Social, and Political Thought. New York: The Macmillan Co., 1956. p 395)

FIFTEEN

WHAT IS SIN?

Simply defined, sin is a state of alienation from God, which shows itself in acts against the will of God, specifically the moral Law of God. It is a matter of common sense to realize there is a variation in gravity of offenses, as is expressed by the Apostle John.

If anyone sees his brother commit a sin that does not lead to death, he should pray and God will give him life. I refer to those whose sin does not lead to death. There is a sin that leads to death. I am not saying that he should pray about that. All wrongdoing is sin, and there is sin that does not lead to death.

(I John 5:16-17)

Mention also should be made that Jesus said that to hate somebody is to murder them in your heart. But there is no record that he ever said that the thought is equivalent to the act. In his teaching, Jesus characteristically went to the spirit and intent of the Law. Therefore, a good case can be made that the Gospel is a spiritualization of the Law.

It is important to note that the ritual of baptism, which is the entrance rite of the Christian faith, is the time when all prior sins are forgiven by God. (Acts 2:38-39) Sins that are committed after baptism are forgiven if they are confessed to God in prayer. (I John 1:9) This process also presumes repentance.

In its consequences, which is a separate concept from guilt, sin has its own built-in motivation to foster repentance, because the old adage seems to be true that,

> The sins you commit two by two,
> you pay for one by one.

In essence, that is in agreement with the maxim,

> You don't break the Ten Commandments;
> you only break yourself upon them.

Some people have to learn that the hard way. You find the evidence of that in wrecked lives, and destroyed families. And the national trend of legitimizing infractions of the Ten Commandments, all in the name of an ill thought out and selfish concept of freedom, has been absolutely disastrous for American society, and probably a prelude to the end of American ascendancy. After all is said and done, there is no gain in waltzing around "the iron in the gospel."

But, there is a very spiritual dimension to baptism, not only in the promises it carries, but also in the ritual of baptism we are marked as one of God's own by the indwelling presence of the Spirit. And I think it gives the capacity to avoid (to the degree that we are willing) the temptations that come through the senses of the body. That vulnerability to temptation, which we inherited from Adam and Eve, is called "natural concupiscence." The propensity of the will to engage in rebellion against the moral will of God comes from the influence of the social environment which is heavily biased in that direction.

As a matter of interest along this line of thought, the famous Mayflower Compact of 1620 was composed in order to avoid rumored mutinous behavior planned by some of the colonists for the time after they landed at Massachusetts Bay. In Puritan theology, if a person was in a covenantal agreement with another person to where it lent support to any sinful behavior, the person thereby shared in the guilt of the sin of the other person. That sharing of the guilt occurs in both Old and New Testaments, and even in modern secular law – aiding and abetting a criminal. That suggests the concept of national guilt, which has sobering implications for many nations, America included.

In Puritan theology there were five covenants, in other words five dimensions of connectedness, which bound each citizen to the rest of the populace. The covenants included theological, church, political, economic, and social covenants. That connectedness, to the point of helpfulness, could bring the wrath of God on all of the colonists, and not just the one who committed the sin, for all or most of them were in consent by lack of action.

As far as alienation from God is concerned, many people blame God for the consequences of their own sins and mistakes, and also when they take the consequences of other people's sins and mistakes, or even natural evil. In the last case, insurance companies typically take a venture into theology and call it an act of God. It is because of that alienation from God that, as St. Paul notes, "God was reconciling the world to himself in Christ." (II Corinthians 5:19)

The world of people needed that avenue of reconciliation to God, for it is a common tendency to blame God, the stars, or somebody, or something beyond ourselves for our sins and failures. But as William Shakespeare aptly stated it:

The fault, dear Brutus, is not in the stars,
But in ourselves, that we are underlings.

(Julius Caesar, I, ii, 134)

There was a couple I met in South Florida who had their house "tented" to kill the subterranean termites, but the company used the wrong gas, and the residual amounts in the carpet and upholstery did irreparable nervous system damage, his more than hers, and he went into depression. One day, just before his wife got home from work, he put a 32 caliber pistol to his right temple and pulled the trigger. The bullet exited his left temple, and in-between it severed both optic nerves. He was permanently blinded in both eyes. But he never lost consciousness until he was given an anesthesia for an operation at the hospital. The next day I got in to see him, and he went into such a rage that he nearly got off of the gurney. Apparently he blamed God for his own mistakes, and like every minister, I was God's representative, and I took the flack. If that man ever decides to be reconciled to God, it is likely to be a long journey home.

> *An example of the sentimentality and unreality that dominate the political opinions of the liberal world is the belief that the power of man's lust and ambitions is no more than some subrational impulse, which can be managed with more astute social engineering or more psychiatric help.*

> (Abraham I. Heschel, "A Hebrew Evaluation of Reinhold Niebuhr" loc. cit., p. 396)

I tell you the truth, all the sins and blasphemies of men will be forgiven them. But whoever blasphemes against the Holy Spirit will never be forgiven; he is guilty of an eternal sin.

Jesus of Nazareth, Mark 3:28-29

SIXTEEN

IS THERE REALLY AN UNFORGIVABLE SIN?

The question most frequently asked of me was, "Is there an unforgivable sin?" And, if so, "What is it?" Jesus, as stated above, was definitely of the opinion that there is such a thing as an unforgivable sin. In the context in which he made that statement, he was accused by teachers of the Law, from Jerusalem, that he was casting out demons by the power of Beelzebub, the prince of demons. But Jesus pointed out that it didn't make any sense, for then Satan's kingdom would fall. Then Jesus made the statement condemning the speaking against the Holy Spirit.

The essence of what is at issue is an inversion of values, calling what is evil, good; and what is good, evil. There could be no excuse for such a reversal of values, for the moral Law of God, summed up in the Ten Commandments, taught what is good and right, as opposed to what is evil and wrong.

89

But the flaw runs deeper than that, to the essence of the soul – to the will, and the inclination of it. On the basis of reported perverse atrocities in crime both in the U.S. and abroad, as well as the extensive atrocities of terrorists, one could justly say that the fault extends to a perversion of the soul, to an orientation of evil.

I remember one man who was a nominal church member (in name only); he was totally non-participating. As part of a yearly financial campaign I went to visit him and told him my reason for coming. He responded by telling me how utterly generous he was in giving to various charities, and it all impressed me as blarney. So I called his hand, "Boy do I have a deal for you! Whatever you give to charities, give it through the church by designating where the money is to go to, and 100% of it will go there. Plus, for tax purposes you will have a copy of the church record of your giving." He immediately became extremely angry and began cursing the Holy Spirit. Why the Holy Spirit was the focus of his wrath is somewhat of a puzzle. I went back to the church office and removed his name from the membership role, lest the judgment of God come upon the church for tolerating such ones in the membership. It was a clear cut case of blasphemy against the Holy Spirit.

A person has to be careful not to presume the place of God. Jesus did not say the person was permanently barred from heaven. Maybe that leaves room for repentance at a later date. But that would take a complete reversal of values, and there is no assurance that is even possible. However, other passages indicate that such an inversion of values of good and evil is permanent. Romans 1:18-32 deals with the subject, and is summed up by this statement,

Furthermore, since they did not think it worthwhile to retain the knowledge of God, he gave them over to a depraved mind, to do what ought not to be done.
                                                              (1:28)

Also, the writer of the Letter to the Hebrews, states essentially the same thing (6:4-12) – that those who by a decision of the will, willfully turn from the faith (apostatize), then there is no longer any forgiveness of sins for them. In effect it says, "Close the door on the way out." It is a fearful thing when a person goes so far wrong that God gives up on him.

I saw one graduate student do something that should be unforgivable, if it isn't already. He had a crucifix on a chain, and was twirling it around his finger while saying, "Hang on, Jesus!" Little wonder that, as one bumper sticker states,

"Jesus is coming again, and boy is he hacked off!"

In Jewish mysticism we often come upon the view that in this world neither good nor evil exists in purity, and that there is no good without the admixture of evil nor evil without the admixture of good. The confusion of good and evil is the central problem of history and the ultimate issue of redemption. The confusion goes back to the very process of creation.

Abraham I. Heschel ("A Heb. Eval. of R. Niebuhr," loc. cit. p. 399)

SEVENTEEN

FORGIVENESS:

WILL GOD FORGIVE US? ON WHAT CONDITIONS? ARE WE OBLIGATED TO FORGIVE OTHERS?

From the perspective of the Christian faith, forgiveness is granted by God on the basis of faith, repentance, and confession in prayer to God. At the time of baptism, the entrance rite to the Christian faith, all prior sins are forgiven. Subsequent sins are forgiven upon confession in prayer to God. (I John 1:9) From the context in which that statement is made (I John 1:5-10), as well as the rest of I John and the New Testament Scriptures, there must be some honest effort at repentance, hard as that may be with minor, habitual sins. But a person must remember that God is street-wise to a hustle.

In Florence, Italy at the Basilica of St. Mary of the Flowers the baptistery is in a separate, circular, marble building with large bronze double doors carved in relief, and called "the Gates of Paradise." It underlines the seriousness of the rite of baptism.

When we turn to God's acceptance of the prayer for forgiveness, we tend to think of the excellent example of it in the Parable of the Prodigal Son. (Luke 15:11-32) In the story the Father represents God, who lovingly welcomes his wayward, sinful son when he returns home penitently. The major theme of the story is God's love for us, even after we are errant and then come home.

But, remember that the Father did not follow the son to the distant country to offer forgiveness; instead he waited for him to come home in repentance before the forgiveness was given. That theme of repentance is the framework of the story in which the major theme of God's love rests.

When it comes to forgiving others, the passage that always comes to mind is the one where Peter asks Jesus the upper limit on forgiveness of his "brother", apparently meaning neighbor. He evidently thought he was showing himself to be generous in suggesting seven times. As the account states,

> Then Peter came to Jesus and asked, "Lord, how
> many times shall I forgive my brother when he sins
> against me? Up to seven times?"
>
> Jesus answered, "I tell you not seven times,
> but seventy-seven times."

(Matthew 18:21-22)

Then follows the famous "Parable of the Unmerciful
Servant" (18:23-35), which reduces down to the binding
principle that "Grace received must be grace passed on."
This principle runs throughout the New Testament, and one
specific application, among others, is that, forgiveness
received from God must be passed on by us in our relations
with other people. Jesus closed the parable by saying,

> This is how my heavenly Father will treat each of
> you unless you forgive your brother from your heart.

(18:35)

There is another crucial factor involved: It is the one
sinned against that can forgive. That is the offended person,
as logic would show, not the observer, or a superficial religious dabbler. Much of the ballyhooed forgiveness by persons not involved in the offense is simply public relations –
and not well thought out.

Strictly speaking, the "obligation" of forgiving
someone who has sinned against you is dependent on their
repentance, for note that Jesus also said,

If your brother sins, rebuke him, and if he repents,
forgive him. If he sins against you seven times in a
day, and seven times comes back to you and says, "I
repent," forgive him.

(Luke 17:3b-4)

Finally, the Lord's Prayer, also called the Our Father,
is highly loaded with meaning in each word and phrase. A
literal translation of the last four lines of petition are:
[Bracketed statements are background information.]

Forgive us our sins,
as we forgive those who sin against us
    [Grace received must be grace passed on.]
And do not bring us to the test,
    [As you did Job, to where faith is on the line.]
But deliver us from the evil one
    [Satan, who did the testing of Job, Peter, and
    the rest of the apostles.]

(Matthew 6:12-13)

Jesus followed this prayer by stating that our forgiveness
from God is conditional upon us forgiving other people.

Life in this world is the time for action, for good works, for worship and sanctification, as eternity is a time for retribution. It is the eve of the Sabbath, on which the repast is prepared for the Lord's Day, it is the season of duty and submission, as the morrow shall be that of freedom from every law. More precious, therefore, than all of life to come is a single hour of life on earth --- an hour of repentance and good deeds, Eternity gives only in the degree that it receives.

Shabbat 30a

EIGHTEEN

WHAT HAPPENS AT THE TIME OF DEATH?

Sometimes in the Old and New Testament Scriptures you see the word "sleep" used in reference to death, but it is pretty obvious that the word "sleep" is just a euphemism, a good word for a bad reality. Otherwise they could simply be awakened. Likewise, there is no use in the Bible of the invented term "soul-sleep." When a person physically dies, the soul or spirit, or in other words the personality, lives on consciously. The brain, a physical organ, is dead, but it was the bridge by which the soul communicated and directed functions in this material dimension of reality. And consciousness, which is a subset of the unconscious, is a reality grid, or filter, that is formed during infancy and before, and imposed on the functioning of the mind in all of its relationships to the material world, including other people.

In the small classic book Return from Tomorrow, by George G. Ritchie, he tells of a tour of the spirit world that Jesus gave him while he was clinically dead. That story inspired Raymond Moody to research and write the excellent book, Life after Life, and then the sequel to it, Reflections on Life after Life. It was a series of accounts of persons who had religious experiences during a period of clinical death. As I recall, most of them spoke of a tunnel with a light at the end of it, and of "spirit guides" who led them toward what appeared to be heaven. A rose by any other name is still a rose. The guides fall in the group of spiritual beings the church has called angels.

The 23rd Psalm is relevant to their experience, particularly verse 4:
> Even though I walk through the valley
> of the shadow of death,
> I will fear no evil,
> for you are with me,
> Your rod and your staff,
> they comfort me.

Not only are guides provided, but they are armed to fend off evil spirits, for the person is one of God's own adopted sons and daughters.

Remember the story of Dives and Lazarus, otherwise known as the Rich Man and the Beggar, and known also as a Parable; however, Jesus told it as a true story: "There was a rich man ..." (Luke 16:19-31) It was the kind of story that was played out in reality every now and then. Notice how it states, "The time came when the beggar died and the angels carried him to Abraham's side. (16:22) The word "angels" is plural, which fits perfectly with the accounts reported by Dr. Raymond Moody, Psychiatrist.

Peter's confession of Christ, and Jesus' response to it is apropos here. (Matthew 16:13-20) Literally translated verse 18 reads:

> And I tell you that you are Peter; and on this rock I will build my church, and the rusty gates of Hades will not screech closed behind it.

In other words, the Christian, because of his solidarity with Jesus, will not hear the gates of Hades close behind him; instead, the person with valid claim to faith goes directly to heaven to be with Christ in a conscious existence in heaven. This is confirmed by St. Paul's remark, "I desire to depart and be with Christ, which is better by far." (Philippians 1:23b) But the grandest confirmation is in the 12th chapter of the Letter to the Hebrews where it speaks of the Christian's life on earth as lived in view of a surrounding cloud of witnesses, including Jesus and all the people of God of prior generations. (12:1-3) Then it says:

> But you have come to Mount Zion, to the heavenly Jerusalem, the city of the living God. You have come to thousands upon thousands of angels in joyful assembly, to the church of the firstborn, whose names are written in heaven. You have come to God, the judge of all men, to the spirits of righteous men made perfect, to Jesus the mediator of a new covenant, and to the sprinkled blood that speaks a better word than the blood of Abel.
>
> (Hebrews 16:22-24)

By the Book, that's it.

Now is the time for judgment on this world; now the prince of this world will be driven out. . . . I will not speak with you much longer, for the prince of this world is coming. He has no hold on me, but the world must learn that I love the Father and that I do exactly what my Father has command-ed me. Come now; let us leave!

Jesus of Nazareth
(John 12:31; 14:30-31)

NINETEEN

WHY DID JESUS HAVE TO DIE?

The question is, Why did Jesus have to die? And the answer typically comes back that the law was that the soul that sins shall die, and Jesus took our place by dying on the cross in atonement for the sins of all mankind. But that still avoids the question, Why did Jesus have to die at all, much less on the cross? After all, God established the law, there-fore he certainly has the power and authority to change it. Then why didn't he? Rather than see his Son go through a horrible, torturous death. Even in the light of God's pro-fessed love for mankind, was the cross really necessary?

The answer to that question is, Yes. Assurances of forgiveness upon repentance, and even tangible proof of God's love, for example in the Exodus, had never been enough for very long. Nor had the assurances of God's love proclaimed by the prophets. But the death of God's Son innocently bearing the guilt of all mankind has proved both convincing and enduring. Once a person believes that Jesus is uniquely Son of God (Divine in nature), and therefore truly God and truly man, then that has both persuasive and enduring power. The idea of his death being for the atonement for the sins of all mankind is believable because it had cost God, and Jesus, a great deal. And yet, it does not violate free will, for in the end the intellectual assent to the truth of Jesus' deity, and commitment of the will to him, is a matter of the person's own inclination of heart.

Everywhere, he saw dim figures seated on the slope, and as he gazed he saw that from a single basket the throng was being fed. ... Then he saw him. The old man was lowering himself to the ground. When he was down and his bulk had settled, he leaned forward, his face turned toward the basket, impatiently following its progress toward him. The boy too leaned forward, aware at last of the object of his hunger, aware that it was the same as the old man's and that nothing on earth would fill him. His hunger was so great that he could have eaten all the loaves and fishes after they were multiplied.

(Flannary O'Conner, The Violent Bear It Away. New York: Noonday Press, 1960. p. 241)

TWENTY

WHY USE BREAD AND WINE IN COMMUNION?

One Friday evening I went to a synagogue service, but the rabbi wasn't there so they held a shortened service. Afterwards I was invited to stay for the fellowship in the foyer, and to share in the Shabbat bread and wine. I asked them why they used those two particular foods, and they didn't know. It was just their tradition. Go into any Protestant church and ask the same question and you will get virtually the same answer to why Christians use bread and wine in communion. Of course, it is commonly known that the bread and wine symbolize Jesus' body and blood in his sacrificial, atoning death. Jesus made that correlation between bread and wine, and his body and blood. (Matthew 26:26-29; Mark 14:22-25; Luke 22:17-20) And because Jesus said to repeat that ritual, it has become tradition to use them in communion. Although wine resembles blood in color, bread doesn't look anything like a body. So, why did Jesus choose those two for the ritual of communion?

As you probably suspect, the answers are closely connected. In the Hebrew tradition and Scriptures, the moral Law of God, summarized in the Ten Commandments (or Ten Words), was the source of salvation to eternal life. The Law was said to be as essential to life as bread; it was the bread of life. The Law was also said to be as sweet as wine. Jesus took those two common, basic foods, which even the poor had, and redirected them to point to himself as the source of salvation, instead of the Law. It was a radical shift in symbolism. Note that, a good case can be made that the Gospel is a spiritualization of the Law. Jesus went to the heart and spirit of the Law in his teaching. Accordingly, he redirected the symbols of bread and wine to point beyond the Law to himself, as the source of salvation. That is in accord with the statement that he is the one through whom God created the world. (Letter to the Hebrews 1:1-4)

Paul the Apostle included some further teachings by Jesus regarding communion (I Corinthians 11:17-32), that whenever they eat the bread and drink the wine, it is to be done in remembrance of Jesus and his sacrificial death. Note, that included is the statement,

For whenever you eat this bread and drink the cup you proclaim the Lord's death until he comes.

Some suggest that since the bread and wine were consumed every evening at supper time at home, then that daily occurrence was a time of remembrance. According to that view, during the first generation of Christians the daily observance was included in the church service (Acts 2:42) and formalized.

One seminary professor told of visiting an Eastern Orthodox church service in Istannbul, Turkey (formerly Constantinople). The sanctuary was elliptical in shape with the altar at the far focus of the elipse. When the people entered the sanctuary they went to the right and followed the perimeter of the sanctuary, viewing the icons and touching the relics, all the while the mass was being said and the incense burned. Then came the receiving of the symbols of communion. Into every sense there was a call to faith: sight, touch, hearing, smell, and finally taste. It was a "presentifying", a making present, an event in the past.

Every communion service functions to some degree as a means of making present the founding event in the past. The concept of the reality of the presence of Christ varies among the various denominations, from simple remembrance of Jesus' sacrificial death in our behalf, to the concept of a change in the substance of the bread and wine into the real physical presence of the body and blood of Christ in the mass of the Roman Catholic Church and the Eastern Orthodox Church. The explanation according to Aristotelian philosophy is that during the mass the "substance," or essence, of the bread and wine are changed into the actual body and blood of Christ, while the "accidents" remain the same – the sensory perceptions: sight, hearing, touch, smell, and taste.

Incidentally, the doctrine of those two churches regarding the presence of Christ in the mass is the one that most fully takes into account all of the teachings by Jesus about communion. Consequently, I think they are more vertical in the orientation in their worship than all of the others. Likewise, the others are more lateral in their orientation in worship than vertical.

The ingesting of the symbols, bread and wine, is in itself a symbolic claim of fundamental unity with Jesus, a taking of him into one's self. Whereas, in previous Hebrew tradition a drink offering was poured out, thereby becoming an irrevocable offering to God.

The "communion" aspect of the ritual is both lateral (with other people) and vertical (with God through Jesus). The latter case is the primary one, because from the very nature of the rite it is a remembering, and therefore is internal and basic. Also, since there is no minimum number of participants specified, there theoretically could be just one person taking communion, and that automatically would trump the lateral dimension. There simply would be no other members to have fellowship with.

There is another aspect of communion that evidently was common in some parts of the early church, at least by the time of St. Augustine. It was the communion with the deceased people of God. The idea comes from the concept that we are surrounded by a great cloud of witnesses," as expressed in the twelfth chapter of the Letter to the Hebrews. According to record, in North Africa in the time of St. Augustine, those seeking to be admitted to the church were asked, "And do you believe that in this church you will attain to the communion of saints?"

As a sidelight, typically the place where a person is most likely to have a paranormal religious experience is in a church building. That is not surprising because a place can be either "profane" or "holy" depending on what happens there. The word "holy" is the translation of a Greek word that means simply "set apart to God." St. Thomas Acquinas, one of the greatest theologians, said one day upon coming out of a mass during his later years, "All that I have written so far is but straw compared to what I have seen in church today!" Reportedly, from then on he wrote lyric poetry.

It is interesting to note that on at least several occasions Jesus alluded to himself as the "living water", which if a person drinks of it he will never thirst again. The moral Law of God was said to be the water of life. The Law was thought to be as essential to life eternal, as water is to life on earth. Again, Jesus was redirecting a symbol to himself. Instead of the Law being the source of salvation, he is the source.

A riddle: *Birds don't fly because they have wings;*
              They have wings because they fly.

Source unknown.

TWENTY-ONE

WHAT IS THE TRINITY?

What's in a name? To make it plain and simple, the word Trinity refers to the triune nature of God as the New Testament Scriptures show him to be: Una Substancia, Tri Persona, or in English, "One Substance, three Persons." That refers to one substance that is divine, or deity, yet three persons. Karl Rahner defined it, three manners of relatedness of the one deity to mankind. At that point a person is really "walking on thin ice." The reason is that it is quite evident, as will be shown later from the New Testament, that the Trinity involves three spheres of consciousness, will, and identity in a very definite and discrete ranking as: God the Father, God the Son, and God the Holy Spirit. The three are bound together by agape, meaning "the unwillingness to do without; love." It is the same bond Christians are called to have to God and to each other as adopted sons and daughters of God, and towards all other people. Honestly put, all of that may stretch the term "monotheism" a bit far; however, there is a unity in being – of the substance of deity. Also, in the "Shema," ("hear"; Deuteronomy 6: 4), the creed of Judaism, repeated twice daily by observant Jews, the first sentence in smooth and interpreted English is: "Hear, O Israel: The Lord our God, the Lord is one." But a literal translation is: "Hear, O Israel: the Lords our Gods is one." There still is mystery associated with the Trinity.

Many people find the concept of the Trinity a little confusing, therefore to use a modern analogy, it is like a triangle. It is all one triangle, but there are three points to it: likewise, there is one substance of deity, yet three spheres of consciousness and will, differentiated by rank as Father, Son, and Holy Spirit. By honest concession, analogy is a form of illustration; it is not a method of proof. It is said that only lawyers and ministers use it as a form of proof.

A better analogy comes to us from antiquity, from St. Augustine (354-430 A.D.), one of the truly great leaders of Latin Christianity. He used the analogy of the mind to explain the Trinity. A person has one mind. The most elemental and basic aspect of the functioning of the mind is memory, and from memory comes reason, and from memory through reason comes will (and love, agape). Likewise, there is one God: God the Father, from whom comes God the Son, and from the Father through the Son, comes God the Holy Spirit.

Throughout the Bible there is a definite and rigid ranking, but still a person must remember that God relates to each Christian by way of love. It is the kindness that only God Almighty is capable of giving. Remember also that it is the "kingdom of God," not the democracy of God, and the people of that era knew of democracy in Greece. Many of the denominations in the U.S. copied the national style of government, rather than the Episcopal in the Bible. The only instance in the New Testament of the manner of selection of elders was by appointment. (Titus 1:5)

In regard to the Trinity having the unity of the same substance of deity, Jesus said, "I and the Father are one." (John 10:30) On another occasion, when Philip asked Jesus to show them God the Father, Jesus' answer was that, "Anyone who has seen me has seen the Father." (John 14:8-14) According to that, if you wish to know what God is like, then read the Gospel accounts of the life of Jesus on earth.

Yet at the same time there is distinct ranking in the Trinity. When asked when he would appear again in glory, Jesus said: "Nobody knows, not even the Son, only the Father." (Mark 13:32) There also is Jesus' statement, "The Father is greater than I." (John 14:28)

All of that is contrary to the apparent understanding of many, who treat the Father and the Son as interchangeable names for the same discrete being. Consequently, they have Jesus praying to God, who by their thinking is Jesus himself. Therefore, they have Jesus presumably talking to himself without realizing it. It is a replay of the ancient heresy of Modalism, where God, appears to mankind first as Father, then as Son, and finally as the Holy Spirit in our time. When challenged, the next step is usually to arbitrarily assert that Jesus was adopted as uniquely Son of God at his baptism. But that gives up the divinity of Jesus; consequently his death would count sacrificially only for himself. Also, an adoption of Jesus is not mentioned in the New Testament. It is worth noting that it would turn out to be a real sink hole for major doctrines of the faith.

After Jesus' resurrection he gave to all of his disciples "The Great Commission," (Matthew 28:16-20) which included the statement by him, "All authority in heaven and on earth has been given to me." (28:18b) That alone is a potent, all encompassing statement when you meditate on the implications of it. He acts as regent for God the Father Almighty who dwells in unapproachable light. (I Timothy 6:14-16)

After many years in the faith amidst the disarray of this world, one pastor stated a riddle,

Birds don't fly because they have wings;
they have wings because they fly.

In other words, from the Christian point of view, it is the will of God that is the supreme determining factor in life. It is the will of God that birds fly, and therefore they have wings. Since God is the supreme determining factor in life, it is our consolation and help that we are united with him by his Spirit within. He is our grounds for life, hope, and for eternity.

Left alone the soul is subject to caprice. Yet there is a power in the deed that purifies desires. It is the act, life itself, that educates the will. The good motive comes into being while doing the good. . . . At the end of days, evil will be conquered all at once: in historic times evils must be conquered one by one.

(Abraham I. Heschel. "A Heb. Eval. of R. Niebuhr." pages 405, 409)

TWENTY-TWO

WHAT WILL HAPPEN AT THE LAST JUDGMENT?

One of the most awesome passages of Scripture, if not the most, is what is called the Parable of the Last Judgment, Matthew 25:31-46; however, rather than being a parable, it is a prophecy that uses an analogy of sheep and goats. Chapters 24 and 25 of the Gospel according to Mathew constitute what is called "the Little Apocalypse." The teachings in those two chapters are in answer to three extremely important questions that the disciples asked. By tradition a rabbi of that time would sit to pronounce his most important teaching. Therefore, Jesus sat to give his answer to these three questions: First, when will the destruction of the temple happen? Second, what will be the sign of Jesus' coming? And third, what will be the sign of the end of the age? (24:1-3) There are several things about his answer that indicates the extreme seriousness of it. The first is that he sits to give the answer; he speaks ex cathedra ("from the chair"), the precedent for the Pope, and probably for modern American secular judges.

Second, from linguistic analysis, detailed in the 1912-1913 volume of the Journal of Theological Studies, it is evident that the Parable of the Last Judgment was spoken in Hebrew, and in free verse poetic form, in the manner of the great classic prophets in the prior history of Israel. When the surviving Greek text is translated into Aramaic a standard text is the result, but when it is translated into Hebrew it falls into the form of free verse poetry in the style of the major prophets. It is evident that Jesus spoke it in Hebrew to underline the utter seriousness of this teaching. Consequently, it is certain that this parable is directly from the mouth of Jesus in unedited form. The very survival and finding of such a text is a gift from God.

There are three major observations in the application of this parable. First, where did he gesture when he used the clause, "one of the least of these brothers of mine." (25:40c) Did he gesture behind him to the people of God already in heaven? (Hebrews 12:22-24) Or did he gesture in front of him to all the nations gathered before him? Through the centuries the church has correctly applied it to all mankind, in harmony with the rest of Scripture. He gestured in front of him.

Second, note there is no mention of faith. We know that Luke had a copy of the Gospel according to Matthew in front of him when he compiled and wrote his account of the Gospel; we know this because of the sections he used verbatim. But Luke chose not to include the Parable of the Last Judgment, evidently because it did not mention faith as a criteria of judgment. Matthew's account of the Gospel is the only one that includes the parable.

Third, the principle by which judgment is rendered is kindness given or withheld to those in need, with a premium on spontaneous kindness, even acts of goodness that were not consciously religious acts. But who then can be saved if judgment is going to be based on manifestations of a person's true self? All of our mitzvahs are flawed. But the act educates the will. We can to a very large degree shape the kind of person we are becoming. Acts of kindness consciously and willfully done form a habit, or pattern of thought, that becomes internalized and spontaneous.

In all fairness the parable seems to imply that some (who thought themselves to be) Christians are also among those being judged. This leads to the conclusion that rather than being based on words – talk is cheap – the saving thing is being like Jesus. It is a consequence of heeding Jesus' call to a higher righteousness (Matthew 5:20) – higher than the moral Law summarized in the Ten Commandments and the ceremonial law. Jesus called people to positive, loving action in addition to the moral Law of God with its requirements to refrain from negative, unloving actions. Consequently the Law of God delivered through Moses constitutes the outer bounds of prohibited action for a Christian. It is the minimum of righteousness.

By decision of the Apostolic Council (Acts 15:22-35) in accord with the Holy Spirit they decreed that Gentile

Christians are freed from the ceremonial law with four rules excepted, and required of all Gentile Christians (Acts 15:29). These are the same four mandates traditionally required of all aliens residing then in the land of Israel. But it makes no specific deletion of the Moral Law.

We can never define obedience in such a way that it can be used against God, and take from him his right of judgment. We can only live in his Spirit, in total commitment, shown in obedience, and dependence on him, trusting in his grace. In that process, the Law, as explained by Jesus serves as a guide.But the attributing of righteousness ("such as we ought to be") comes as a gift from God because of, and by faith -- that whole-hearted commitment to God through Christ. Therefore the primary element is the relationship to God.

The ironic thing is that on one occasion of Jesus' lament over Jerusalem, he said of the temple,

> Look, your house is left to you desolate. I tell you, you will not see me again until you say, "Blessed is he who comes in the name of the Lord."

> (Luke 13:35)

In reference to the temple being desolate, it refers to it being bereft of the Spirit of God – God forsaken – because of the killing of prophets sent to Jerusalem.

Jesus' call to a higher righteousness, to a spiritualization of the Law, is in keeping with his statement,

> Not everyone who says to me, "Lord, Lord," will enter the kingdom of heaven, but only he who does the will of my Father who is in heaven.
>
> (Matthew 7:21)

In other words, there has to be integrity to the claim of faith. A person's manner of life must be in accord with the claim of faith they make.

In writing about the appearance of Christ in glory, the Apostle Paul states that divine retribution is coming on those who trouble Christians.

> This will happen when the Lord Jesus is revealed from heaven in blazing fire with his powerful angels. He will punish those who do not know God and do not obey the gospel of our Lord Jesus. They will be punished with everlasting destruction and shut out from the presence of the Lord and from the majesty of his power on the day he comes to be glorified in his holy people and to be marveled at among all those who have believed. This includes you, because you believed our testimony to you. (II Thessalonians 1:5-10)

Notice that he names two groups for punishment. First, "those who do not know God." They did not look into the matter, even though they could know from nature that there is a God, and he is powerful. Second, "and do not obey the gospel of our Lord Jesus." They heard it, but rejected it in fact if not also in word,

Their punishment is exclusion from the presence of the Lord. They had not wanted anything to do with him anyway, and so the Lord is just rubber stamping their decision. He continues his respect for free will. Their punishment is exclusion from the presence and light of the Lord – to the outer darkness, where there reportedly is weeping and gnashing of teeth. It is a place of unrestrained evil, for it lacks the moderating presence of the Holy Spirit that is in us and around us. Unmitigated evil truly is hell; that is in contrast to the comic book concept that is prevalent.

In <u>Paradise Lost,</u> by John Milton, the pain of hell is the anguish of Paradise lost. That is in accord with Scripture and with the early church fathers.

In Florence, Italy in the Medici Chapel where many of the Medici princes are buried, in one room there are three life-size statues by Michelangelo. A statue of Mary holding the infant Jesus stands in front of the west wall and faces east. In front of the north wall and facing south is a statue of a Medici prince, limply holding a scepter, indicating the weakness of his rule. In front of the south wall the third statue faces north. It is of a Medici prince who tightly grasps a money box, which indicates his known avarice. Although both of those statues stand opposite each other, they both have their faces turned toward the statue by the west wall. They look to their salvation, the infant Jesus.

There the statue of Mary holds the infant Jesus, but she does not look down at him. She looks distantly to the east, as if in anticipation of when he comes again in glory.

Funeral Oration for Chief Francis Godfroy
1788 to 1840
friend and advisor of Frances Slocum

Brothers, the Great Spirit has again taken to himself another of our once powerful and happy, but now rapidly declining nation. The time was when these forests were once filled with red men. But the same hand whose blighting touch has withered the majestic frame that lies before us and caused the noble spirit that animated his body to seek another abode has in like manner dealt with his fathers and with ours. And so it will deal with us. Such occasions as this have become so common recently that we scarcely notice them longer. But when the brave and generous are stricken, our tears of sorrow flow freely.

Our brother was brave and generous, and as a tribute to his virtue and a reward for his goodness, the tears not only of his own people but also of many of the white people flow freely. The poor will weep at this event for at his table they were wont to feast and be happy. The weak will mourn because his power was ever directed to their protection. But he has left this earth of vexation and sorrow and is now enjoying with Pocahontas and with Logan the joys that the Great Spirit has prepared for those who do well and faithfully their duty. Brothers let us follow his example and practice his virtues.

by Wa-pa-pin-cha, aka George Hunt, from <u>Among the Miamis</u>, Indians of Indiana, Ohio, and Michigan.

(cf., <u>The Lost Sister Among the Miamis</u>. by Otho Winger. Elgin, Illinois: Elgin Press, 1936. page 135)

TWENTY-THREE

WHAT ABOUT PEOPLE
OF OTHER RELIGIONS?

According to the New Testament it seems they will be judged by their own law, apparently at the time of passing to the next phase of life. (I Peter 1:13-17) That judgment is an initial judgment that determines whether they go to Hades, or to the considerably less desirable habitat in Gehenna, otherwise known as hell. A small, very readable book on the subject of hell is <u>The Great Divorce</u>, by C. S. Lewis.

In the Parable of the Last Judgment, the sole criteria of judgment was kindness given or withheld to those in need. By that rule it seems that many then would enter heaven, to join the Christians already there. However, there is a caution on seeing the two judgments as distinct and separate events. Time – the sequentiality of events, the one-after-anotherness of events – is a strictly this worldly phenomenon, a ratio between mass and speed. There appears to be a different form of sequentiality in the realm of the spirit.

It seems to be implied in the Letter to the Hebrews that the call to faith went out to all people in many and various ways. That would be consistent with the statement that God's will is for all people to come to repentance and life eternal with him. (II Peter 3:8-9) Consequently, the historic universal appeal is contained in the statement,

> In the past God spoke to our forefathers through the prophets at many times and in various ways, but in these last days he has spoken to us by his Son, whom he appointed heir of all things, and through whom he made the universe. The Son is the radiance of God's glory and the exact representation of his being, sustaining all things by his powerful word.
>
> (Hebrews 1:1-3a)

Not surprisingly, Christians are also judged – for reward, not with salvation hanging in the balance; for that is already secured by admission to heaven on the basis of a valid life of faith.

It is interesting to note that in the Beatitudes (Matthew 5:1-12), all of them except three have their reward in the future; those three are the first one, and the last two. In those three the present tense is used; the reward is immediate – a place granted and reserved now in the kingdom of heaven. A valid translation of the first one is,

> Blessed are those who know their need of God, for theirs is the kingdom of heaven.
>
> (5:3)

That is a great consolation.

I have told you these things, so that in me you may have peace. In this world you will have trouble. But take heart! I have overcome the world.

Jesus of Nazareth, (John 16:33)

TWENTY-FOUR

DOES GOD GUARD THE LIVES OF CHRISTIANS?

The answer, oddly enough, is yes, with the circle of protection varying in diameter as needed for the moral development of the individual, in the light of what is best for all concerned in the perspective of eternity. Trouble and suffering properly borne builds moral character by breaking down pride, the basis of all sin. In Christian theology pride refers to the inordinate love of self more than God and more than others. According to Hebrews 12: 1-13, it is proof that we are truly sons and daughters of God, in that he takes the trouble to discipline us for our own good, just as we do our own children. He usually does it with a velvet glove.

Not that God causes us trouble, he doesn't need to. All he has to do is withdraw his protection a measured amount. There are two really good examples of that measured protection in the Bible.

119

In the case of Job, God uses him as an example of true righteousness.

> Then the Lord said to Satan, "Have you considered my servant Job? There is no one on earth like him; He is blameless and upright, a man who fears God and shuns evil."
>
> (Job 1:8)

In other words, he worships God and leads a moral life. To make a long story short, Satan states that it is no wonder, after all you have given him everything. But take what he has and see if he doesn't curse you. But, when it is done, with the very important restriction by God that Job himself is not to be touched, Job still remains loyal to God. When this is pointed out to Satan, he replies,

> Skin for skin! A man will give all he has for his own life. But stretch out your hand and strike his flesh and bones, and he will surely curse you to your face.
>
> (Job 2:4-5)

Then comes a terrible sickness upon Job, followed by an extensive set of monologues and dialogues. Near the end of the treatise the Lord demands of Job,

> Brace yourself like a man;
>   I will question you,
>   and you shall answer me.
>
> Would you discredit my justice?
>   Would you condemn me to justify yourself?

> Do you have an arm like God's,
> and can your voice thunder like his?
> (Job 40:7-9)

In other words, some of God's decisions and actions are beyond human understanding, and remember who you are dealing with and show respect.

The second case is in the New Testament. At the Last Supper Jesus said,

> Simon, Simon, Satan has asked to sift you as wheat. But I have prayed for you, Simon, that your faith may not fail. And when you have turned back, strengthen your brothers.
> (Matthew 22:31-32)

Notice that Satan could not get a crack at Peter, nor the others, without permission from God. The circle was drawn. God is our shield and defender, our ever present help in time of trouble.

I think that protection is extended to all of the people who live by faith. I am so bold as to venture that among my own experiences, when I was eighteen I totaled an automobile and walked away without a scratch or bruise. On another occasion, when I was thirty-seven, I found myself in a very deadly situation. To make a long story very short, in spite of good logic and calculation – but based on some very bad information – I was alone in the pitch darkness of a heavily overcast night at the bottom of the Grand Canyon, on a trail that varied from one to three feet wide, and was about 100 feet above the roaring Colorado River. The trail was on the face of a cliff, and in at least one place it had collapsed away and was just gravel with a distinct slope toward the river below. I had no flashlight because I had no reasonable expectation of being on the trail at night.

If I had known the danger that awaited me at the end of the trail, I don't know that I would have had the faith and courage to go on. The trail ended at a footbridge over violent rapids of the river at least 50 feet below. I knew ahead of time that the bridge was there, my last ordeal before reaching Phantom Ranch in a box canyon. What I didn't know ahead of time was that about every other one of the expanded metal grates that were the flooring of the bridge were tilted so that if a person stepped on them, he would slide through to the rapids below. The only way to cross the bridge was to hold tightly onto the flanking cables that supported the bridge, and carefully step over the tilted sections – which involved constantly looking down in order to correctly place my feet, all the while seeing the roaring rapids below. That certainly ranked among the most tense times in my life, and of sustained fervent prayer.

On another occasion during an automobile trip, certain, unavoidable death in just a moment was upon me, and by sheer miracle I was delivered. I chalked it up to the grace of God, and as an indication that God was not finished with my work in this phase of life, for I didn't have time to pray.

There were other occasions of deliverance that fit under the statement found in one Colonial Era diary,

> Between the saddle and the ground,
> Mercy I asked, and mercy I found.

See that you do not look down on one of these little ones. For I tell you that their angels in heaven always see the face of my Father in heaven.
Jesus of Nazareth, Matthew 18:10

TWENTY-FIVE

WHAT IS THE STATUS OF CHILDREN?

In the above quotation the word in the Greek is correctly translated as angels. It is not the one for spirit or soul. That statement by Jesus is a great consolation to myself, and I am sure to other parents as well. Children are a true treasure in this world. It is a comfort to know that they are under God's care and concern, and if worse comes to worse in this mean world shot through with sin and grief, they are safe in the arms of Jesus.

The story came to me second-hand, from a woman who knew the mother. She was in the hospital after giving birth to an infant. She awoke to see two angels standing by the bed, and she immediately began weeping at the thought that they had come for her, and she would be leaving her husband to care for and raise the infant. Her husband came in then, but she couldn't compose herself enough to convey what was happening. Fearing something had happened, he immediately left for the nursery. She saw the angels follow him out of the room, and she went to pieces again thinking the angels had come for him. She would be left alone to raise the child. But when he reached the nursery, the infant stopped breathing. The father was a dentist and was able to give the infant cardiac resuscitation, but to no avail. The angels had come to take her home to heaven; they were a delegation to take her safely and fearlessly through "the valley of the shadow of death." So help us God and his holy gospel.

A person might consider that story as a bit maudlin; however, although I have no evidence for it, the story is exactly as it was told to me by a friend of the mother. In the face of such heart wrenching events we can only trust in the goodness, mercy, and kindness of God the Father Almighty. It seems that the basic principle God uses for such a decision is, "What is the best for all concerned in the perspective of eternity?" Very often it is not what we would have decided, except perhaps in retrospect. Also, no one, but God alone, knew what tragedy, grief, or devastation lay ahead for the girl. That God allowed (not caused) an early demise to come upon her may have been a great act of mercy.

If perchance we go through "the dark night of the soul," when events cause misfortune to the extent where we have nothing left to go on except faith itself, we have to be careful that we don't stumble at faith's greatest test. And we pray with renewed significance the Lord's Prayer, the Our Father, especially where it says in the literal translation, "And do not bring us to the test, but save us from the evil one." The test alluded to is the ultimate test, where faith itself is on the line, as in the case of Job.

Note that the prayer is recited in the first person plural, so that when we are stressed to the point of being unable to say the words, the others include us by praying using "our" and "us."

To turn to a strictly positive account, when my daughter was about one and a half years old, I noticed her tipping a glass of water over the edge of a bathroom counter-top. I spontaneously called her name to warn her away. Perhaps I startled her to where she lost her grip; whatever the case, the glass slipped from her hands, and shattered on the tile floor. She slipped on the wet tile and fell face down in the pieces and shards of glass (some of them two inches long). I screamed for my wife as I ran to help my daughter. I was terrified that 911 might not get there in time to save her life. I picked her up carefully, and turned her over before I placed her on the bed on her back. I was totally astounded to see that she was unharmed. To come out of that event without injury was absolutely impossible, yet she did. Surely by God's grace, she must have a guardian angel looking after her.

I have come to appreciate the practice of infant baptism by some communions. At baptism there is the gift of the Holy Spirit dwelling within (Acts 2:38); that provides a marking of the person as one of God's own, and therefore under his care. Baptism functions as an entrance rite, a historical marker established in place and time. Afterwards, if plagued by guilt, the Christian can say with confidence, "I am baptized!"

There are several places in the New Testament that speak of the meaning of baptism, but not one place that states the importance of the form or the age at which it can be done. Pronouncements on that are human doctrines that often are in effect a means by which churches are split so that one person can rule a new denomination. It must be noted that the meaning of the Greek word transliterated as baptism means to dip, and as a result immersion is the most illustrative.

Many Protestant churches encourage their youth to be baptized at about the age of twelve, after the Jewish tradition of the Bar Mitzvah, the coming of age of a boy to responsibility, to manhood. In the secular aspect of society in America and Europe, the Roman Empire divisions of age ranges generally applied until recently. According to their tradition, infancy is age zero to seven; seven to fourteen is childhood; and fourteen to twenty-one is youth. At age twenty-one, the youth came of age. I think we should have kept that system.

There is in I Corinthians 7:14 the clear basis for what the Puritans called "Federal Holiness." In that concept, as stated in the text cited, through a believing (Christian) spouse, an unbelieving spouse and underage children are sanctified, or holy (such as one ought to be). In other words, because of, or in deference to, one believing spouse, the immediate family is under the care and protection of God.

"We do not know with what we must serve until we arrive there." (Exodus 10:26) All our service, all the good deeds we are doing in this world, we do not know whether they are of any value, whether they are really pure, honest or done for the sake of heaven - until we arrive there – in the world to come, only there shall we learn what our service was here.

Rabbi Isaac Meir of Germany
("A Hebrew Evaluation of Reinhold Niebuhr", Idem p. 40)

TWENTY-SIX

DO THE PEOPLE OF GOD UNDERGO JUDGMENT?

Apparently after an initial determination that the person has a legitimate claim to faith, there is a judgment for reward. As one old saying goes,

In heaven, everybody's cup will be full,
But not everybody's cup will be the same size.

The sobering thing is that the Apostle Paul in his writing to the Christians at Corinth, and speaking of all Christians, stated,

> For we must all appear before the judgment seat of Christ, that each one may receive what is due him for the things done while in the body, whether good or bad.
>
> (II Corinthians 5:10)

There is an allusion to such a judgment in I Corinthians 3:10-15, where it speaks of each man's works will be tried by fire [judgment] to test the quality of the work – to determine if there were any unworthy motivations. Even if none of what he did survives the fire of judgment, the person will survive, saved. In this world where we are often in jeopardy, it may seem that there is no end to it. But then we must remember:

> For God so loved the world that he gave his one and only Son, that whoever believes in him shall not perish but have eternal life. For God did not send his Son into the world to condemn the world, but to save the world through him.
>
> (John 3:16-17)

That can be our consolation, for we don't seek justice, but mercy through the redeeming atonement through Jesus. He didn't come to worry everybody to death, but for our salvation.

One French philosopher stated, "I don't know whether or not there is eternal life, but let us live so that it will be an injustice if there isn't."

"Asher, Asher," the Rebbe said softly. "This world has not been kind to you."

I sat very still. He shook his head slowly "Everything is in the hands of heaven, except the fear of heaven." he quoted. "What can I tell you my Asher? I do not know what the Master of the Universe has waiting for us. Certain things are given, and it is for man to use them to bring goodness into the world. The Master of the Universe gives us glimpses, only glimpses. It is for us to open our eyes wide."

from <u>My Name Is Asher Lev</u>, by Chaim Potok. (Greenwich, Conn.: Fawcett Publications, Inc., 1972, p. 270f)

TWENTY-SEVEN

WHY NOT JUST LIVE ETHICALLY INSTEAD OF BEING CHRISTIAN?

According to Christian doctrine there are some very good reasons to be a Christian, rather than going it alone and hoping to pass muster on Judgment Day. Of course some do not bother with it because they thereby save paying the 10% tithe that is the obligation of every Christian. Some join a service club, wrongly believing it to be an equivalent substitute. But in either case, it fails to recognize the obligation of worship of God and the celebration of communion with the remembering and gratitude for Jesus' atoning death in our behalf.

129

There are definite advantages to including one's self in the kingdom of God as a Christian. They are:

1) Forgiveness for all prior sins now, rather than waiting and trusting to luck on Judgment Day. Note that subsequent sins can be forgiven upon repentance and confession in prayer.

2) There is the assurance that eternal life is a present time possession, rather than a hope and dream for the future.

3) Adoption as a son or daughter of God comes at the time of baptism, the entrance rite into the Christian faith. This status is far more than the metaphorically speaking status of son or daughter of God that every individual has as a right because of being human.

4) There also is the gift of the indwelling of the Holy Spirit, which can be thought of as an extension of the Spirit of God within, or a share in the Divine life – as grace is sometimes defined.

5) Life on this earth is lived under the blessing and care if God.

6) And always there is the presence and love of God, where God's love [agape] is an unwillingness to do without. That is a great consolation in this day and age.

There use to be a TV commercial that reminded us that we only go around once in this earthly phase of life.

Therefore, for a single throw of the dice the Christian faith has the best odds of maximizing happiness – for eternity.

Another thing, the principle upon which judgment will be based at the Last Judgment is kindness given to those in need or withheld, with a premium on spontaneous kindness. In other words, it is what is expected of any Christian.

For me there is only the traveling on the paths that have a heart, on any path that may have a heart. There I travel, and the only worthwhile challenge for me is to traverse its full length. And there I travel – looking, looking, breathlessly.

> by Carlos Castaneda.
> The Teachings of Don Juan,
> A Yaqui Way of Knowledge.
> (New York: Pocket Books, 1968. p. 195)

TWENTY-EIGHT

WHAT IS MEANT BY THE PEACE OF GOD?

In order to receive peace from God, a person must be at peace with God, reconciled, no longer alienated from God. It seems there are many people who allow themselves to be beaten down or even defeated by the vicissitudes of life, as evidenced by one manner of escapism, rampant drug addiction. Also for some who are bearing the consequences of sin because of the moral grain to the universe, there often is alienation from God.

Most people's complaints against God are not that severe. Typically they blame God for any negative event or factor in their life, anywhere from a fender bender to not having achieved their ambitions in life. One way or another it nearly always turns out to be a bum rap on God, except in the rare case when he acts in righteous judgment. In the 1980's there was a case of that in Miami, Florida that was reported in the news. An armed man entered the Sunday morning church service of a small, poor congregation that was meeting in a store front. At gunpoint he ordered a collection be taken of all the money they had. When that was done, it wasn't enough to convince him that it was all they had, and he ordered a second collection. Then he died of a massive heart attack. Apparently it was instant retribution!

I don't think God needs to cause trouble when there can be beneficial effects from it; all he needs to do is back off on his protection a measured amount, because trouble or suffering properly borne builds moral character by breaking down pride, the basis of all sin.

A good rule to follow in going through the valleys of life, is to not admit the existence of problems, for the word problem has a negative connotation. Instead, use the word challenges, which is a positive word that carries an inherent call to action. It's just like in snow skiing; it is absolutely crucial to lean forward on the skis, otherwise a fall is certain. Likewise, it is vitally necessary to lean into life. Live every day all the way up and all the way down. And turn every defeat into an opportunity for victory. Using that rule, and with the help of God, it is a winning combination.

Obviously, there are both winners and losers in many of the endeavors of life. Professor James Glass stated, "There is a tried and true theological principle in life, that every stick has two ends, consequently you grab it in the middle. You look for the compromise." However, when it comes to religion – morality and eternity – it is a you bet your life proposition. Half way measures are inappropriate. What is required is primary commitment, a basic orientation in life commensurate with the higher righteous that Jesus calls us to. It is a life long living out of the old parting blessing, "God be with you," now contracted to a generally secular wish, "Good-bye."

There is an interesting story in Luke 8:42b – 48 It occurs in Mark 5:24b – 34 of a woman who had a hemorrhage for 12 years, continually seeking healing from doctors, but to no avail, and the expenditure of all her money. She came up behind Jesus, thinking if she could only touch his garment she would be healed. As soon as she touched his clothes, she felt the bleeding cease.

Jesus asked aloud who touched him for he felt the power go out of him.

> Then the woman, knowing what had happened, came and fell at his feet and, trembling with fear, told him the whole truth. He said to her, "Daughter, your faith has healed you. Go in peace and be freed from your suffering."
>
> (Mark 5:33-34)

If you translate it literally, then the two sections of interest read: "Daughter, your faith has saved you. Go into peace." The dominant meaning of the clause "Your faith has saved you," is eternal life. The word translated "saved," is appropriate. The healing had already taken place earlier. It is anticlimatic to strain the meaning to refer to the healing.

The other word of concern is very legitimately translated as "into" instead of "in," for that is characteristically the meaning of the word in the Greek. There is another Greek word that almost solely means "in." Consequently, when Jesus said to her, "Go into peace," he was not just expressing a wish for her safety on the way home. Rather, he was pronouncing the blessing of a new and fulfilled state of being in this world, characterized by: tranquility of soul, concord, every kind of blessing or good, benediction, and good wishes. In short, it was a second blessing of a very high order, well worth going back for.

In our day, some Christians receive that kind of fulfillment early on in the journey of faith; for others it remains a process of growth. Both ways are a gift by the goodness and mercy of God. As St. Augustine would say, "It is a constant turning towards God." And the journey of faith is very definitely the way with heart.

In the year 1643, when all things throughout the nation were demolished or profaned, Sir Robert Shirley, Baronette, built this church, whose singular praise it is to have done the best things in the worst times, and hoped them in the most calamitous.

Inscription on the
dedication stone of
a church in England.

PROJECTIONS REGARDING THE FUTURE

Looking ahead to what the 21st century will hold, and with no claim to be a prophet, there are some factors that are not normally noted. Recognition of these is a matter of bearing in mind the old joke that what this country needs is a one-armed economist (rather than one who says, on the one hand this, but on the other hand that). Futurists typically assume that what is happening now will happen forever, or at least for the fore-seeable future. Presumed psychics (ones without a true gift of prophecy) read the news magazines and make educated guesses about the near future, which nearly anybody can do with at least equal success.

In one sermon, just three months after I had begun as minister of a church, on New Year's Sunday I reminded the congregation of the above observations, and told of the time I heard Jean Dixon speak before a high school assembly. In the question and answer period, one student asked her to make a prediction right there and then. She looked angry, but then conceded to do it; she said, "There will be a great earthquake next year." Without time, date, and location it was a sure thing, because every year there is a great earthquake some place. I told the congregation that any of us could do just as well, and I predicted a great earthquake for that very year. The next morning Kobe, Japan was leveled by an earthquake, and the next Sunday an elder of the church asked me to not make any more predictions. My prediction was a fluke in timing. I am neither a prophet nor the son of a prophet – although there probably have been other comments on my lineage.

One very alarming factor operating silently in the background, as the future becomes the present, is the fact that the genetic pool is degrading, yet it is the most precious possession of mankind for it involves our very humanness. Back in 1964 I was talking to a professor of biology at the University of Maryland and commented that on the basis of my readings on the biological effects of radiation, I had come to three conclusions. First, the background radiation is the wind that makes evolution go. Second, the human race is de-evolving, because natural selection no longer applies, and third, that process has been in operation for about two thousand years or more. Note that it gives new meaning to the frequent line in the Old Testament, "I am no better than my fathers." Would that modern people were as perceptive as they were. A case in point is that there was not a single individual of the 20th century (Albert Einstein included) who was as brilliant as Sir Isaac Newton; he was simply beyond modern scales of intelligence.

The professor told me that I was correct on all three points, and that the U.S. Government was in the process of freezing sperm from select men so that in the future, 100 or 1,000 years hence, the race could be rejuvenated – but only the sperm could be frozen and used then for restoration. As of that time they could not yet freeze the eggs in a manner in which they could be revived. About in the middle 1980's there was a very brief public notice that there had been a way developed to preserve the eggs indefinitely for future fertilization and propagation.

Another peril in the offing is "emergent intelligence" in computers, especially when it is considered in the context of nano-mechanics, bio-engineering, and molecular computers. The combination could be deadly, as Michael Crichton illustrates in his book titled, Prey. Reportedly some of the most powerful computers, on their own, have developed characteristics such as passive or aggressive. And two of them connected together have a capacity greater than the sum of the two.

But the more immediate threat, that has now been in operation for at least half a century, is the destruction of the family. It is a trend that has been facilitated by the court system's endorsement of a corrupted concept of freedom so that it is inherently selfish and fosters a "me first" mentality, and is dedicated to the idea that sexual climax is the highest good that a person can aspire to, and constitutes the most basic human right. It is sometimes referred to as "the New Age Morality", whereas it should be more correctly called "the Old Age Morality", for all of the various perversions mentioned are found in stories in the Old Testament.

Lastly, another factor that adds an ominous note to the future is the frequency in recent history of genocide. Evolution-wise, mankind came on the scene as an armed killer, a fact that the U.N. hasn't seemed to take into consideration. As one poet wrote, "The leaves have fallen, and so has mankind." In addition, television and motion pictures are amazingly effective in changing both attitude and behavior, as is witnessed by the fact that business and industry spend billions of dollars each year for television advertising on that proven principle as witnessed by the realities of commerce.

And every year many people throughout the world become increasingly brutal, coarse-minded, and foul-mouthed, thanks to the incredible efficiency of modern media; culturally it is a leveling down, not up. It is logical to conclude that as a consequence, many nations are becoming less governable. Of course, any nation can be ruled out of the barrel of a gun, as has been shown many times, such as by Cuba. May God spare us from a dictatorship becoming the dominant manner of government.

I have developed a saying, "What is real is what is, not what people say is real or true." A common equivalent statement is, "It isn't necessarily so." It is well worth keeping in mind in this so-called information age, deluged by trivia and disinformation, and where truth and worthwhile principles are a rarity, there is the sobering reality of the proliferation of weapons of mass destruction that remains an increasing threat to all of us.

It was predicted by one man in 1904 that the 20th century would be noted for volcanic change. He was right. I think that the 21st century will be noted for genocide, and secondly pandemics; that seems to be the emerging trend in world events.

But remember how Jesus said that there would be repetition of wars and rumors of war and famines and earthquakes. The one distinctive thing about the end time, he said, was that because of the increase of sin, the love among people for one another would grow cold. I see that happening now.

In my own lifetime I have seen an amazing devaluation of human life throughout the world and even in the United States of America. As an extreme example, take for instance the execution by starvation of Carol Shriver by the court system and the state of Florida. She was conscious and guilty of no crime but it was decided that her life was not worth living, therefore using straight talk, and calling an ace an ace, she was executed by starvation, which is a slow and painful death. This is sin of a very high order. There also is the alarming probability that the U.S. leads the world in infant sacrifice, especially true in near-term abortion. It usually, if not always, appears to me that the motivation of the mother is to save money. The natural next step of that national sin of abortion is the increasing homicide rate on children. That is already in process. And the consequences of those sins will come home to roost someday. As one evangelist I used to know would say, "Payday some day."

Looking down the road, reason seems to indicate an extremely high likelihood of the U.S. becoming involved in a nuclear war, or at least some weapon of mass destruction. And it will be a war at least regional in extent, probably the Middle East. The catastrophe will come because of a lack of recognition of the nature of the conflict between good and evil. I pray that I am wrong.

But whatever the future holds, we have the consolation that for those who live by faith, by the will of God, underneath are the everlasting arms. And one fine day, history will come to a halt before the throne of God.